The Wanton Seed

The Wanton Seed

English Folk Songs from
the Hammond and Gardiner Manuscripts

Originally selected and edited by Frank Purslow
Revised by Malcolm Douglas and Steve Gardham
with notes by Steve Gardham

Francis
Boutle
Publishers

This edition published by Francis Boutle Publishers
272 Alexandra Park Road
London N22 7BG
Tel: 020 8889 7744
info@francisboutle.co.uk
www.francisboutle.co.uk

Published in collaboration with the South Riding Folk Network

First edition copyright © English Folk Dance and Song Society 1965

This edition © Francis Boutle Publishers 2015
Original selection and notes copyright © the Estate of Frank Purslow
Introduction and notes copyright © Steve Gardham

ISBN 978 1903427 98 9

Contents

Malcolm Douglas 1954–2009

This new edition of *The Wanton Seed* is dedicated to the memory of Malcolm Douglas. It has been made possible through generous subscriptions from organisations and individuals, many of whom were counted amongst Malcolm's friends and colleagues.

The Traditional Song Forum

Dr Mike Stannett

Hedingham Fair

South Riding Folk Network

Hallamshire Traditions

The Folklore Society

Pete Coe

Ron & Jenny Day

Anita Allen

David Eyre

John & Enid Scholey

Peter Smith

Martin Watson

Sheffield City Morris Men

Doc Rowe

Paul Sartin

Tony Cunningham

Derek Schofield

Robert Taberner

Martin Graebe

Tony Wilson

Bryony Griffith, Will and Jonah Hampson

Dr Arthur Knevett

Alec & Margaret Thompson

Bryan Ledgard

Bright Phoebus Collective

Ryburn 3-Step

Jeff Warner

Jim and Georgina Boyes

David Stenton

Lizzie Dye

Professor Ian Russell

Jack Crawford

Dave Kidman

Phil Heaton

Carla Ribeiro-Dawson

Chris Willans

Bob Butler

Carol Schofield

Mike Wild

Doug & Jane McCallum

The Sompting Knucker

Felicity Greenland

Sheila & Vic Gammon

Soundpost Community Network

Russ Clare

Vikki Appleton-Fielden

Pauline Cato

Nine Daies Wonder

Acknowledgements

The late Malcolm Douglas revised *The Penguin Book of English Folk Songs* for reissue by EFDSS as Classic English Folk Songs in 2003. He maintained extensive websites for the South Riding Folk Arts Network, Yorkshire Folk Arts and the *Folk Music Journal*, and was graphic designer for *Stirrings Magazine* (folk and acoustic music in the South Yorkshire/North Derbyshire region) and the Sheffield Folk Festival. Under the alias J.T. Dogg he was also a noted illustrator and cartoonist.

Steve Gardham (as "Dungbeetle") wrote the series "A Veritable Dungheap", examinations of the role of the broadside ballad in the evolution of folk song, which began in English Dance & Song and continues at the *Musical Traditions* website: http://www.mustrad.org.uk/. He is Chair of the Yorkshire Garland Group, a web-based archive of traditional song in Yorkshire. Steve also worked closely with Malcolm Douglas on the preparation of the reissue of Marrow Bones, the first in this series.

David Atkinson is the editor of the *Folk Music Journal* and author of *The English Traditional Ballad: Theory, Method and Practice* (Aldershot and Burlington, VT: Ashgate, 2002. The third edition of his *English Folk Song: An Introductory Bibliography Based on the Holdings of the Vaughan Williams Memorial Library* (2006) is available on the EFDSS website. He is a member of the team preparing a critical edition of the James Madison Carpenter Collection of Traditional Song, Music and Drama, with special responsibility for textual editing.

Special thanks are due to Malcolm Taylor, previously the librarian of the Vaughan Williams Memorial Library, and his colleagues Elaine Bradtke and Peta Webb, for their help with the explorations of the Hammond and Gardiner collections.

Steve Roud, for his invaluable Folk Song and Broadside indexes, and for kindly providing copies of some hard-to-find material. Bob Askew and Tim Radford for sharing the results of their historical and genealogical researches.

Julian Elloway for his initial preparation of the music. Graham Pratt for his musical and technical expertise in preparing the files for printing.

The late Frank Purslow, for the original *Wanton Seed* and for his unfailing patience and good humour when faced with interminable questions on points of detail.

David Atkinson, for editorial advice, the broadside bibliography, and for making available to us his editing notes formulated for use on the Carpenter Collection.

Dr Mike Stannett, for rescuing the original files from Malcolm's computer.

Preface

When *Marrow Bones* was first published, the folk song revival was rapidly expanding and a whole new generation was becoming aware of the rich heritage of English traditional music. The problem for singers was where to find it, and that was what prompted Frank Purslow to edit an accessible selection of songs from the Hammond and Gardiner manuscripts, which duly appeared as *Marrow Bones* in 1965. Three more volumes followed – *The Wanton Seed* in 1968, *The Constant Lovers* in 1972, and *The Foggy Dew* in 1974 – and Frank Purslow's little volumes are fondly remembered and still sought after to this day, though they have been out of print for some time.

EFDSS published a revised edition of *Marrow Bones* in 2007. Malcolm Douglas had agreed to edit the whole series; however, recognizing that with all of the fresh information now available and the sheer number of songs involved, this would be a marathon task, Malcolm asked Steve Gardham to share the load. Together, they embarked on two week-long stints in the Vaughan Williams Memorial Library working on the original manuscripts, this being before the Hammond and Gardiner manuscripts became available online, as part of the EFDSS's Take 6 project at <http://library.efdss.org/archives/>.

Due to other commitments, Steve Gardham was obliged to relinquish the project after the first book was published, and Malcolm Douglas continued to work alone on the second book, *The Wanton Seed*. Malcolm had completed checking the manuscripts and was just about to start on the notes when he was diagnosed with terminal cancer – a devastating blow to all who knew him. This was particularly felt in the world of folk song research where he was acknowledged as one of the most thorough and helpful researchers of his generation.

When Steve heard the news, he determined to continue Malcolm's work and took on the task of completing what he had started. We are very grateful to Steve for making this publication possible.

Introduction
to the new edition

THE ORIGIN OF THE SONGS

Looking through the notes of the first editions of all four volumes in the *Marrow Bones* series, one cannot fail to notice that even then (1965–74) Frank Purslow was well aware that nearly all of the songs had appeared in street literature – broadsides, chapbooks, sheet music, cheap anthologies, and the like – at some time; and indeed that a significant number of them had filtered down from the eighteenth-century theatres and pleasure gardens, most likely via the same medium. Since those first editions were published, collections of street literature have become much more accessible to researchers, so it is now possible to say that at least 85 per cent of the songs appeared at some point in this medium; and it is quite likely that a further 5 per cent did likewise but have not yet surfaced or else have been lost due to the ephemeral nature of such publications.

There is also a growing number of researchers – myself included – who have studied the earliest examples of each ballad and believe that the vast majority of them actually originated as street literature, although it is now impossible to demonstrate this point with total certainty. Undoubtedly, there is plenty of evidence, from the late eighteenth century onwards, that there was a constant two-way flow between oral tradition and cheap print, which brought about widely varying versions of the same ballad, sometimes even issued by the same printer. However, some of the more marked variation is very likely down to rewriting by the broadside writers.

More than 10 per cent of the English corpus of oral ballads can be traced back in some form to sixteenth- and seventeenth-century broadsides, which were largely printed in the old gothic type known as 'black letter'. The market for ballads in this period, during which printing was a relatively expensive process, was largely among the growing middle ranks of society, such as tradesmen and their apprentices; but those in positions of power also used the medium for political purposes, and some of them, such as Samuel Pepys, actually collected broadside ballads. Those ballads printed during this period that survived into the twentieth century in oral tradition did so mainly because they continued to be printed in later centuries, adapted to meet current fashions (see 'Betsy the Serving Maid' in this volume). However, a few apparently continued in oral tradition without the aid of print, *The Duke's Daughter's Cruelty*, of c.1690–96 (Pepys Ballads 5.4) being probably the best example, which thrived in oral tradition in various forms throughout the English-speaking world as 'The Cruel Mother' (Child 20; *Marrow Bones*, p. 26). Another example, *The Country Cuckold; or, The Buxom Dame's Frollick in a Field of Rie, with her Lusty Gallant*, also of c.1690–96 (Pepys Ballads 4.139), was only known until recently from the repertoire of Harry Cox of Norfolk, who called it 'The Barley and the Rye'; however, another fragment has recently been recorded from Travellers by one of our youngest folk song collectors, Sam Lee.

One feature that occurs during this period, and which died out in later centuries, was that of printers occasionally including the initials of ballad authors on their broadside sheets. The most celebrated were Martin Parker (fl. 1624–47) and Laurence Price (fl. 1628–75), who both wrote ballads that were later found in oral tradition. Parker, for example, wrote the song 'John and Jone' in 1634, which eventually became the ballad 'John Appleby' (see *Marrow Bones*, p. 56); while c.1657 Price wrote 'The Famous Flower of Serving Men' (Child 106) (see Pepys Ballads 3.142; *The Constant Lovers*, p. 34). They also contributed a Robin Hood ballad each to Child's *English and Scottish Popular Ballads* (Child 154 and 147). Many of the ballads of this period were so popular that they continued to be printed in the eighteenth century and some, like those included in Thomas D'Urfey's *Wit and Mirth; or, Pills to Purge Melancholy* (1719–20, and various earlier editions), were anthologized and revised and reprinted numerous times, demonstrating that the songs and ballads continued to be popular with those who could afford relatively expensive books.

A relatively new phenomenon that had arisen by the middle of the eighteenth century was the printing of long ballads, many of them based on continental stories and folktales or older historical legends. These were printed on broadsheets in four or five columns, with up to sixty stanzas, by printers such as the Dicey firm of Northampton and London, and Turner of Coventry. While few of these ballads survived in their entirety in oral tradition, the more popular ones were later drastically rewritten, with far fewer stanzas, to cater to a mass market provided by increasing literacy and social mobility, coupled with improved technology leading to cheaper printing. One example can be found in the third book in this series, *The Constant Lovers*, at p. 91. under the title 'The Silk Merchant's Daughter'. Nineteenth-century versions. commonly titled 'New York Streets', usually have eleven stanzas, whereas the early eighteenth-century broadside titled *The Female Champion* has thirty-three (British Library, 11621.b.3.(6.)).

The ballads were rapidly becoming the province of the common people and the middle classes were moving on to supposedly more sophisticated entertainment in the pleasure gardens and theatres. However, even the flowery outpourings of these venues eventually filtered down to the broadside trade, and a significant proportion eventually entered oral tradition, such as 'Bright Phoebus' in this volume. Pastoral songs of this sort are easily recognizable for they often contain superfluous descriptions and classical allusions, as is evident in numerous hunting songs of this type.

By the end of the eighteenth century, the longer ballads were still being printed in the form of booklets or pamphlets, which are known as 'garlands' and 'songsters'; but even more important for the spread of the ballads among the common people was the move to printing shorter versions on single 'slips', one ballad on a flimsy narrow piece of paper. These would be hawked in the streets by a ballad singer/seller, or 'chaunter', who would sing the latest ballad as he sold copies, which he would have bought in bulk from the printer. It was in this way that the vast majority of our English oral corpus first saw the light during the late eighteenth and early nineteenth centuries. Most were written by specialists at the bottom of the scale of poets, broadside writers or (as they are sometimes termed) 'hacks'. They would then take their productions to the printer, who would give them a shilling per song. Of course, these writers, when devoid of original inspiration, were crafty enough to take an existing ballad and rewrite it, with perhaps a new slant and a new first stanza and title, and the printer would willingly accept it as 'A New Song'. In this way, the most popular ballads started to appear on stall copies in widely varying forms, some even hybridized from more than one ballad. In addition, ballads could find their way back into print from oral tradition. Although these broadside writers are largely anonymous, one John Morgan was afforded the privilege of having his name printed with his ballads, and a few of his pieces, such as 'Caroline and her Young Sailor Bold', entered oral tradition (see *The Foggy Dew*, p. 12).

By the early nineteenth century, the trade was reaching its peak and the most popular form of stall copy became the two-column broadside. More than half of the ballads under discussion cannot be traced back any further than the presses of James Catnach and John Pitts in London, who dominated the medium when the trade was at its height from about 1800 to 1840. Ballads based around the American and continental wars abound, along with the themes of poverty and transportation. During this period the fashion for love songs, songs of parting, and songs of deprivation, endowed with a strong sentimental slant, blossomed. We often refer to this trend as Victorian, but the theme was popular long before the queen came to the throne.

The ballads printed by Pitts and Catnach and their contemporaries continued to be issued by their immediate successors and by the rapidly proliferating provincial presses in towns and cities around the country. With the coming of the railways, bringing faster communication and the migration of labour, the same ballads were printed with little variation across the land and, indeed, across the English-speaking world. This was far from a one-way process centred on London. Many Irish ballads came into England via Liverpool with the immigrant labourers (see, for example, 'The Lake of Colephin' in this book). After 1840, when the immensely popular American minstrel troupes toured the country, their songs were quickly snapped up by the broadside printers as well as being printed as sheet music. Many of their tunes entered oral tradition, both as songs and as dance tunes.

Just as in the eighteenth century, many of the songs from the theatres and pleasure gardens found their way on to street literature. New sources of commercial songs also found their way on to broadsides, including popular songs of the period and songs from the supper rooms and beer cellars of London, such as 'Sam Hall', which was popularized by W. G. Ross (for an oral version see *The Constant Lovers*, p. 42). Songs from the glee clubs, where members of the urban middle classes gathered to perform short songs in harmony in trios and quartets using sheet music, also found their way on to broadsides. From this source come pieces like 'Dame Durden' and several others found in the repertoire of the Copper family of Sussex.

Another phenomenon from earlier centuries which reached its peak in the nineteenth century was burlesque. This involved taking a well-known ballad and delivering it on stage in a comic manner. Sometimes this meant altering the words into exaggerated dialect, sometimes parodying the original; but more often very little of the original was altered and emphasis was placed on a comic delivery, taking advantage of the fast scene-shifting that occurs in traditional ballads. 'Lord Lovel' (Child 75) and 'Barbara Allen' (Child 84) were both given this treatment, and broadside ballads such as 'William and Dinah' and 'William Taylor' likewise suffered the same ignominy. In the first decades of the nineteenth century the celebrated clown Joseph Grimaldi was the master of this style, but it really reached its peak towards the middle of the century with such household names as J. W. Sharp, Fred Robson, and Sam Cowell. The best-known example is undoubtedly 'Villikins and his Dinah', the burlesque of 'William and Dinah' which first featured in Henry Mayhew's 'burletta' *The Wandering Minstrel*. Both the burlesque and the original were widely printed on broadsides, and both survived side by side in oral tradition, and the tune became one of our most ubiquitous folk melodies (an oral version of 'William and Dinah' is given in *The Constant Lovers*, p. 110).

By the mid-nineteenth century, mass entertainment was beginning to take a foothold with all classes in the form of the music hall. The most astute of the printers, such as the Glasgow Poet's Box, were encouraging all and sundry to bring into their printing offices any songs that were already becoming popular, including the latest pop songs. In this way, the latest songs were printed even before they could be published in the more expensive sheet music format, typically with colourful lithographs of the artistes in character on the cover. In this way, many of the more popular pieces entered into oral tradition. When the collectors of the late nineteenth century started to record oral traditions, these songs were (understandably) largely ignored, even while the collectors pounced on the earlier broadside ballads, with a particular interest in their tunes. However, one artiste of the period – not, strictly speaking, a music hall performer, but a concert favourite with the more polite – was Harry Clifton (1832–72), many of whose songs appear in folk song collections, and some of which are still sung today. In this volume are two of his songs, 'The Country Carrier' and 'Watercresses', and 'The Unfortunate Tailor' is in *Marrow Bones*.

By the end of the century, the popularity of these ephemeral sheets was waning fast, though a few long-established printers continued to print them well into the twentieth century. Most people could now afford to buy full books of songs; audio recordings were beginning to appear; and, in the urban areas, the young were becoming more attracted to the latest music fashions. The older songs continued in oral tradition in conservative rural areas, which is where the collectors largely recorded the songs that appear in this series of anthologies.

An extended version of this introduction, which includes copies of some of the original sheets, can be viewed at www.tradsong.org/where_that_song.pdf

STEVE GARDHAM
May 2015

The Songs

ABROAD AS I WAS WALKING (THE DISTRESSED MAID)

Tune: GG/1/13/781, Sarah Goodyear, Axford, Hampshire, August 1907.
Text: GG/1/10/589, Alfred Porter, Basingstoke, Hampshire, September 1906; final stanza from GG/1/13/781.

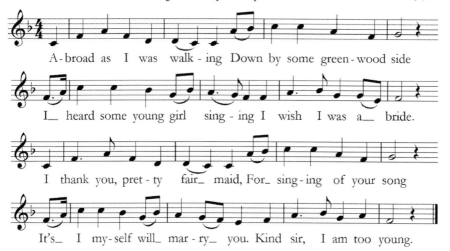

A-broad as I was walk-ing Down by some green-wood side
I— heard some young girl sing-ing I wish I was a— bride.
I thank you, pret-ty fair— maid, For— sing-ing of your song
It's— I my-self will— mar-ry— you. Kind sir, I am too young.

Abroad as I was walking
Down by some greenwood side
I heard some young girl singing
I wish I was a bride.
I thank you, pretty fair maid,
For singing of your song
It's I myself will marry you.
Kind sir, I am too young.

The younger you are the better
More fitter for my bride
That all the world may plainly see
I married my wife a maid.
Nine times I kissed her ruby lips
I viewed her sparkling eye
I catched her by the lily-white hand
One night with her to lie.

All the fore part of that night
How we did sport and play
And all the latter part of that night
I slept in her arms till day
Till day, till day, till day
Till daylight did appear.
The young man rose, put on his clothes
Said, Fare you well, my dear.

What did you promise me last night
As I lay by your side?
You promised you would marry me
Make me your lawful bride.
What I did promise you last night
Was in a merry mood
I vow, I swear, I do declare
I'm not so very good.

Go down to your father's garden
Sit down and cry your fill
And when you think on what you've done
You blame your forward will.
My parents brought me up
Like a small bird in a cage
And now I am with child by you
Scarce fourteen years of age.

It's other farmers' daughters
To market they do go
But I, poor girl, must stay at home
And rock the cradle o'er
To rock the cradle o'er and o'er
Sing hush 'ee, lullaby
Was there ever a maid and a pretty fair maid
In love so crossed as I?

ALL THROUGH THE BEER (GOOD BROWN ALE AND TOBACCO)

GG/1/9/496, Charles Chivers, Basingstoke, Hampshire, August 1906.

Oh where is my hat, oh my nobby, nobby hat
The hat which I wear in cold weather?
For the brim is wore out and the crown is kicking about
And the lining is gone to look for better weather.

Chorus: *It was all through the beer, the jolly, jolly beer*
It was all through the beer and tobacco
For I spent all my tin with the women a-drinking of gin
And across the briny ocean I must wander.

Subsequent verses follow the same pattern as the first:

Coat / collar / fronts / sleeves
Waistcoat / breast / back / collar
Breeches / waist / legs / arse
Shirt / collar / sleeves / tail
Stockings / toes / heels / legs
Boots / uppers / soles / laces

ALL UNDER THE NEW-MOWN HAY

HAM/3/13/19, William Gulliver, Alresford, Hampshire, March 1906.

As I was going over the fields
Mark you well what I do say
As I was going over the fields
A fair pretty lass came close to my heels

Chorus: *Which caused me to go a-screwing*
And brought me to my ruin
Which caused me to go a-screwing
All under the new-mown hay.

When nine long months was over, you see
Mark you well what I do say
When nine long months was over, you see
She placed a little one on my knee.

Chorus: *Oh no more I'll go a-screwing*
For that has been my ruin
No more I'll go a-screwing
All under the new-mown hay.

And now this child will want a nurse
Mark you well what I do say
And now this child will want a nurse
Which causes me to pull out my purse.

Chorus: *Oh no more, etc.*

And now this child must go to school
Mark you well what I do say
And now this child must go to school
Or else he'll die a natural fool.

Chorus: *Oh no more, etc.*

And now this child is like to die
Mark you well what I do say
And now this child is like to die
I am so sorry I cannot cry.

Chorus: *Oh again I'll go a-screwing*
For that's not been my ruin
Again I'll go a-screwing
All under the new-mown hay.

And now this child is dead, you see
Mark you well what I do say
And now this child is dead, you see
There's plenty more beer and tobacco for
me.

Chorus: *Oh again, etc.*

THE BARLEY RAKING

Tune: GG/1/16/989, Mrs Hall, Axford, Hampshire, October 1907.
Text: GG/1/3/80, Henry Godwin, Twyford, Hampshire, June 1905; stanza 3 amended and stanza 4 added from a broadside by Fortey, London (British Library, 11621.h.11, vol. 7, no. 339).

'Twas in the season of the year when hay it was a-making
And harvest now was coming on and the barley wanted raking
So this young couple they did agree all for to have a jovial spree
All for to have a jovial spree amongst the barley raking.

Chorus: *Rite tal le la la rel li gee wo*
Sing fal le la la rel li gee wo
All for to have a jovial spree
Amongst the barley raking.

After eight long months was gone and past this poor girl fell a-sighing
After nine long months was come and gone she fell a-heavy crying
She wrote a letter to her love saying, O my dear and turtle-dove
Will you return to your true-love to ease her of her aching?

He took the letter in his hand and on it stood a-gazing
He took the letter in his hand and on it stood amazing
He took the pen and wrote again, To think of me it's all in vain
For a married life I do disdain, so well do I like my freedom.

I have got a good pair of shoes as ever was made of leather
I cock my beaver up in front and face both wind and weather
And after that I have run my race and cannot find a better place
I will return to your sweet face, we'll live and love together.

'Twas down in handy Liverpool if I am not mistaken
'Twas down in handy Liverpool where this young man was taken
He told the magistrate so free, the child did not belong to he
You rogue, you rascal, then said she, remember the barley raking.

BEDLAM (THROUGH MOORFIELDS)

GG/1/6/282, Moses Blake, Emery Down, Lyndhurst, Hampshire, June 1906, augmented from a Disley of London broadside (BL 11621.b.11.1.156).

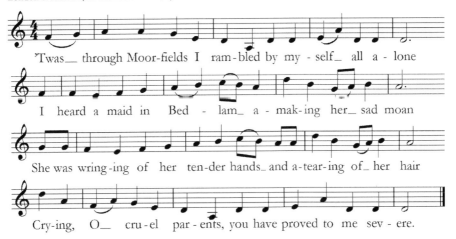

'Twas through Moorfields I rambled by myself all alone
I heard a maid in Bedlam a-making her sad moan
She was wringing of her tender hands and a-tearing of her hair
Crying, O cruel parents, you have proved to me severe.

It's all through my own true-love, your apprentice boy, you know
You forced him to the seas which has proved my overthrow
This sad disconsolation which makes me to complain
Crying, Oh shall I ever see my own true-love again?

'Twas early the next morning this young sailor came on shore
He walked and he talked down 'longside of Bedlam door
He overheard his true-love most grievously complain
I'm afraid I shall never see that young lad I love again.

The sailor he looked round him and stood in surprise
Then peeping through a window he saw her lovely eyes
He gave to the porter a large piece of gold
Saying, Show me to my wife, she's the joy of my soul.

And when that the sailor this young damsel did see
He took her off her strawy bed and set her on his knee
Are you that young man that my father sent to sea?
Or are you come hither to make a fool of me?

Oh yes, I am the young man that your father sent to sea
And I have now returned all for the love of thee.
Then if it be so, all my sorrows they are fled
I'll bid adieu unto these chains and this cold strawy bed.

THE BED-MAKING

Tune: HAM/5/36/9, Marina Russell, Upwey, Dorset, December 1907.
Text: HAM/4/25/3, George Udall, Halstock, Dorset, June 1906; amendments from GG/1/11/648, Benjamin
Arnold, Easton, Winchester, Hampshire, November 1906.

Oh my father he was a good old man
He sent me to service when I was young.
My missus and I we never could agree
Because that my master he would love me.

My missus she sent me all up aloft
To make up her bed both neat and soft
My master followed after with a gay gold ring
Saying, Betsy, take this for your bed-making.

My missus came upstairs all in a great haste
And caught master's arms all around my waist
From the top to the bottom she did him fling
Saying, Master, take that for your bed-making.

Oh first in the kitchen and then in the hall
And then in the parlour around the ladies all
And they all asked me where I had a-been
I told them, Up aloft a-bed-making.

My missus she turned me out of door
She called me a nasty impudent whore
And the weather being wet and my shoes being thin
I wished myself back at the bed-making.

When six months were over and seven months past
This pretty little maid grew stout about the waist
She could scarcely lace her stays nor tie her apron string
And then she remembered the bed-making.

When eight months were over and nine months were gone
This pretty little maid bore a lovely son
She took him to the church and had him christened John
And sent him home again to this gay old man.

BETSY THE SERVING-MAID (BETSY THE SERVANT MAID)

HAM/5/11/1, Robert Barrett, Puddletown, Dorset, September/October 1905.

The graz-ier's daugh-ter liv-ing near A_ fair young dam-sel as you shall hear

Then_ up_ to Lon-don she did go___ To_ seek for ser-vice as you shall know.

The grazier's daughter living near
A fair young damsel as you shall hear
Then up to London she did go
To seek for service as you shall know.

Her master having but one son
Oh she being fair, his heart she won
Oh Betsy being so very fair
She drawed his heart into a snare.

One Sunday evening he stole her thyme
Unto young Betsy he told his mind
By all the swearing powers above
'Tis you, fair Betsy, 'tis you I love.

His mother then being standing nigh
Hearing these words that her son did say
Next morning by the break of day
Unto fair Betsy she took her way.

Saying, Rise up, rise up, my fair Betsy
And dress yourself most gallantly
For in the country you must go
Along with me for one day or two.

As they was a-crossing over the plain
They saw some ships sailing over the main.
No wit, no wit could this poor woman
   have
But to sell poor Betsy to be a slave.

In a few days after the mother returned.
O welcome, mother, replied the son
Come tell me, tell me true, I pray
Where is young Betsy? Behind, you say?

O son, o son, I plainly see
What love you bear to poor Betsy
Your sobbing and sighing are all in vain
For Betsy's a-sailing across the main.

In a few days after her son lie sick
No sort of music his heart could take
But he often did sigh and often cry
O Betsy, Betsy, I shall die.

In a few days after her son lie dead
Mother wrung her hands and she tore her
   head
Saying, If I could fetch but my son again
I'd send for Betsy far over the main.

BETTER FOR MAIDS TO LIVE SINGLE

GG/1/7/405, George Lovett, Winchester, Hampshire, August 1906.

O you maids that do mean to get married
I pray look before you do leap
For fear that a fool or a sloven
Like me you might happen to get
If he's either one or the other
He's just like the lad I have got
And for fear you should think that I love him
I'll give him the name of Watch Pot.

Chorus: *So it's better for maids to live single*
Than marry a miser like me
Until I get rid of my darling
Contented I never will be.

He sits at home at my elbow
For work he has nothing to do
He peeps in each hole and each corner
I can keep nothing out of his view
He watches every bit that I swallow
He's worse than a rat-catcher's dog
He turns up the pots and the dishes
And roots about just like a hog.

The other day we had bacon and cabbage
And little of that was my share
All the while he was eating the bacon
Straight in my face he did stare
Why didn't you bring in more bacon?
There isn't enough for us two
But I'll leave you a bit of green cabbage
I think that is better for you.

If to stirabout he takes a liking
To thicken the pot he won't fail
And while that the water is boiling
He'll eat four or five pounds of raw meal
Come leave out my supper a-cooking
Put milk in the pot and be quick
For indeed I intend to scrape it
When I have done licking the stick.

BLOW THE CANDLE OUT

Tune: GG/1/16/1040, George Gregory, Hartley Wintney Union, Hampshire, October 1907.
Text: GG/1/16/1040; stanza 3 from GG/1/16/1009, George Whiteland, Preston Candover, Hampshire,
October 1907.

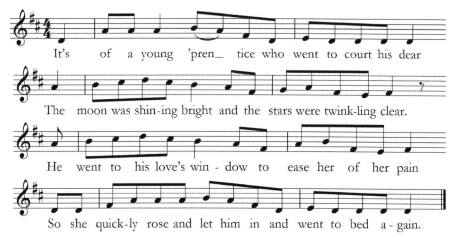

It's of a young 'prentice who went to court his dear
The moon was shining bright and the stars were twinkling clear
He went to his love's window to ease her of her pain
So she quickly rose and let him in and went to bed again.

My mother will be angry if she comes to know
My father will be angry and prove my overthrow
I would not for five guineas that he should find it out
So it's take me in your arms, my love, and blow the candle out.

Your father and your mother in yonder room do lie
Embracing one another and so will you and I
Embracing one another without any fear or doubt
So it's take me in your arms, dear, and blow the candle out.

'Twas early the next morning before the break of day
This young man rose, put on his clothes, and was for going away
But she was loth to part with him but dare not speak it out
So it's take me in your arms, my love, and blow the candle out.

When nine months were over, nine months and a day
He wrote to her a letter that he was going away
He wrote to her a letter without any fear or doubt
And he told her that he'd never return to blow the candle out.

THE BLUE COCKADE (THE WHITE COCKADE)

Tune: HAM/4/22/1, Edwin Bugler, Beaminster, Dorset, June 1906.
Text: HAM/4/22/1; augmented from GG/1/9/538, David Clements, Basingstoke, Hampshire, August 1906;
GG/1/18/1126, Richard Moore, Hampshire, [n.d.]; HAM/2/2/9, Mrs Gulliver, Combe Florey, Somerset, May
1905; GG/1/10/564, David Marlow, Basingstoke, Hampshire, September 1906; GG/1/14/844, James Pike,
Portsmouth Workhouse, Hampshire, August 1907.

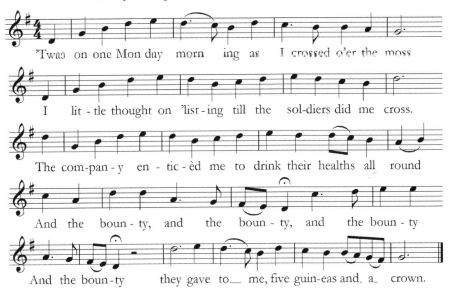

'Twas on one Monday morning as I crossed o'er the moss
I little thought on 'listing till the soldiers did me cross
The company enticed me to drink their healths all round
And the bounty, and the bounty, and the bounty
And the bounty they gave to me, five guineas and a crown.

So early the next morning, 'twas by the break of day
Our captain he gives orders for us to march away.
Then into your ranks and files, boys, all on your native shore
Fare thee well, fare thee well, fare thee well
Fare thee well, my dearest Polly, girl, I never shall see you more.

My head being full of liquor, love, I didn't think of you
But now I'm forced to go and join the orange and the blue
My dear, be of good cheer while I march over the plain
Then I'll marry, love, I'll marry, then I'll marry
Love, I'll marry you, sweet Polly, when I return again.

Then he pulled out his handkerchief to wipe her flowing eye
He says, Leave off your weeping, likewise your mournful cries
Here is my hand and here's my heart, there's no other girl but you
Oh I wish that, oh I wish that, oh I wish that
Oh I wish that I had never joined the orange and the blue.

Oh I hope you'll never prosper, I hope you'll always fail
And everything you takes in hand, I hope you won't do well
And the very ground you walks upon, may the grass refuse to grow
Since you've been, since you've been, since you've been
Since you've been the cause of my sorrow, grief, and woe.

It's true my love is 'listed and wears the blue* cockade
He's a proper handsome tall young man, likewise a roving blade
He's a proper handsome tall young man, he's gone to serve the queen**
Whilst my very, whilst my very, whilst my very
Whilst my very heart is breaking all for the loss of him.

I'll go down to yonder valley and there I'll sit and sigh
I'll sit and sigh for my false love until the day I'll die
'Pon every tree I'll write his name to let the whole world know
That he's been, that he's been, that he's been
That he's been the cause of my sorrow, grief, and woe.

or white, green, black, etc.
**or king.*

THE BOATSWAIN AND THE TAILOR

Tune: GG/1/19/1196, Henry Blake, Bartley, Hampshire, September 1908.
Text: GG/1/15/965, James Channon, Ellisfield, Hampshire, October 1907; chorus from GG/1/19/1196.

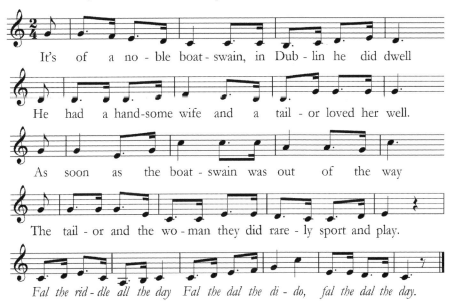

It's of a noble boatswain, in Dublin he did dwell
He had a handsome wife and a tailor loved her well.
As soon as the boatswain was out of the way
The tailor and the woman they did rarely sport and play.

Chorus: *Fal the riddle all the day*
Fal the dal the dido, fal the dal the day.

The boatswain he came home so late one night
So loudly he did holloa, so boldly he did shout
He waked the poor tailor out of his sleep
And he says, My loving woman, wherever can I creep?

My husband has a chest which stands hereby
In it you may creep and so cunning you may lie.
And while you lay there be sure to stay still
There you are so safe as a mouse in a mill.

The boatswain's wife went downstairs to open up the door
And there she saw her husband and one or two more
Oh then she saluted him all with a kiss
She says, My loving husband, how long you have been missed.

I'm sorry to disturb you and rob you of your rest
He says, My loving wife, I'm a-come for the chest
These fellows being so stout and so very strong
They took up the chest and they carried it along.

Before that they came to the top of the town
The heft of the chest made the sweat come trickling down
One said to the other, We'll put it down to rest
For damme, I am sure that the devil's in the chest.

Oh no, it's no devil, you need not to fear
For it's I, the little tailor, and thee has brought me here.
Since I have brought thee here, I will pack thee off to sea
Thou shall not stay at home to make a cuckold of me.

THE BOLD DRAGOON

Tune: GG/1/5/275, Moses Blake, Emery Down, Lyndhurst, Hampshire, May 1906.
Text: GG/1/5/275; stanza 4 from GG/1/16/1003, Mrs Hopkins, Axford, Hampshire, October 1907.

My father is a lord and a lord of high renown
And if I marry a soldier 'twill pull his honour down
So my birth and your birth it never will agree
So take it as a warning, bold dragoon, said she.

A warning, a warning, I never means to take
I'll either wed or die, love, for thy sweet sake.
These words that he said made the lady's heart to bleed
So they both went to church and got married with speed.

As they had been to church and returning home again
They met her honoured father and seven armed men.
I fear, said the lady, we both shall be slain.
I fear not at all, said the jolly dragoon.

March on, my dearest jewel, here is no time to prattle
Don't you see I am well armed, just fitting for the battle.
So the dragoon drawed his cutlass which made the bones to rattle
And the lady held his horse while the dragoon fought the battle.

Oh hold your hand, the old lord said, bold dragoon, hold your hand
And you shall have my daughter and ten thousand pounds in hand.
Fight on, said the lady, my portion is too small.
Oh hold your hand, bold dragoon, and you shall have it all.

Come all you pretty fair maids that have got gold in store
Never despise a soldier although he's mean and poor
For a soldier is a man that will fight for his own
Here's a health to our king* and his jolly dragoon.

*or queen

BONNY KATE

GG/1/16/1027, William Burgess, Titchfield, Hampshire, September 1907.

'Twas at New-mar-ket you shall hear— There did dwell a dam-sel fair.

'Twas at New-mar-ket you shall hear— There did dwell a dam-sel fair.

Some they called her Bon-ny Kate Go-ing to— Com-ing from New-mar-ket late.

'Twas at Newmarket you shall hear
There did dwell a damsel fair.
'Twas at Newmarket you shall hear
There did dwell a damsel fair.
Some they called her Bonny Kate
Going to
Coming from Newmarket late.

Oh oft-times a lawyer she did meet
Who enticed her with kisses sweet (*bis*)
He enticed her more and more
Showed her gold
Showed her gold and silver store.

Oh it's if you will sleep in town
These five guineas I'll put down. (*bis*)
She took him then to the sign of The Bell
Where in service
Where in service she did dwell.

Can I have a bed, said he
For my wedded wife and me. (*bis*)
Oh yes, kind sir, the landlord said
No, nor he did not
No, nor he did not own his maid.

Can I have a supper dressed
Fish and fowl of the best (*bis*)
And a bottle of wine to drink a while
For young Kate
For young Kate has walked a dozen mile.

After supper the glass went round
Until the score came to one pound (*bis*)
That the lawyer freely paid
Now to bed
Now to bed, young Kate, he said.

Young Kate she was handed on before
And at the top there was a door (*bis*)
Young Kate she went straightway through
That's where she bid
That's where she bid the lawyer adieu.

Lord, how this lawyer stamped and swore
When he found he'd lost his dear (*bis*)
And young Kate's heart was crowned with
    joy
To think she'd got
To think she'd got five yellow boys.*

eighteenth-century slang for golden guineas

THE BOY AND THE HIGHWAYMAN (THE CRAFTY PLOUGHBOY)

HAM/4/27/10, George Vincent, Corfe, Dorset, November 1906.

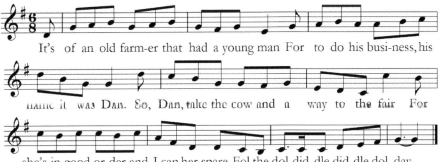

It's of an old farmer that had a young man
For to do his business, his name it was Dan.
So, Dan, take the cow and away to the fair
For she's in good order and I can her spare.

Chorus: *Fol the dol diddle diddle dol day.*

So the boy took the cow to the fair in a band
And very soon got there, as we understand
Soon after he got there he met with three men
And sold them the cow for six pounds and ten.

They went to the alehouse to have them some drink
Where the men they paid the boy all the chink
There sat an old highwayman drinking his wine
Said he to himself, That money'll be mine.

The boy took his leave and away he did go
The highwayman soon followed after also
And soon overtook him all on the highway
You're well overtaken, young man, he did say.

How far are you going this way? he did say
How far are you going along this highway?
Three or four miles further from what I do know.
Come, jump up behind and away we will go.

They rode till they came to some very dark lane
When the highwayman said, I must tell you plain
Deliver your money without any strife
Or else I will certainly take your sweet life.

He pulled open his coat and the money pulled out
And on the green grass he strewed it about
When the highwayman was picking it into his purse
To make him amends, Dan rode off with his horse.

The highwayman shouted and bade him to stay
But Dan never heeded but kept on his way
And back to his master safe home he did bring
Horse, saddle, and bridle, a very fine thing.

They open the saddle-bags, there they behold
Five hundred pounds in bright silver and gold
Besides two brace of pistols, I'll swear and I'll vow
Dang it! says Dan, but I've well sold the cow.

Says his master to Dan, For your courage so bold
Three parts of the money you shall have in gold
But as for that villain, it served him quite right
To have put upon him a Yorkshire boy's bite.

BRIGHT PHOEBUS

GG/1/16/1031, Henry Brown, Hartley Wintney Workhouse, Hampshire, October 1907; text slightly amended as per original composition by James Hook.

Bright Phoebus has mounted the chariot of day
While the hounds and the horns call each sportsman away
Through meadows, through fields, with speed they now bound
While health, rosy health, is in exercise found.

Chorus: *Hark away! Hark away!*
Was the word to the sound of the horn
And echo, blithe echo
And echo, blithe echo
Makes joyous each morn.

Each hill, each valley so lovely to view
While poor puss flies for cover and the dogs quick pursue
Behold, there she flies o'er the wide-spreading plain
While the opening pack quick pursues her amain.

At length puss is caught and lies panting for breath
And the shouts of our huntsmen give the signal for death.
What joys can compare to the sports of the field?
To hunting all pleasures and pastimes must yield.

THE BROKEN-DOWN GENTLEMAN

GG/1/6/310, George Blake, St Denys, Southampton, Hampshire, June 1906.

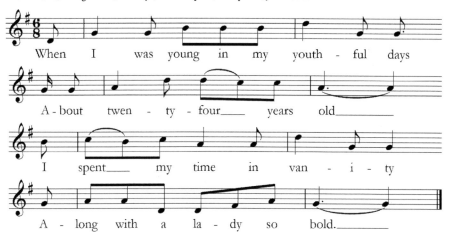

When I was young in my youthful days
About twenty-four years old
I spent my time in vanity
Along with a lady so bold.

I wore the ruffles at my wrists
A cane all in my hand
No farmer's son could with me compare
All over the nation so grand.

I kept a pack of hounds, my boys,
With servants to wait on me
For I did intend my money to spend
And that you may plainly see.

I kept a coach and six bay horses
With hangers all round about
With a golden tassel on each horse's head
Just ready for me to ride out.

I steered my course to Epsom, boys,
Horse racing for to see
'Twas there I spent ten thousand pounds
All in the light of day.

I steered my course back home again
My purse it did run small
And I was a broken-down gentleman
And that was the worst of it all.

My landlord he came for the rent
Of bailiffs there came three
They took away all that I had
And swore that they would have me.

The rogues and thieves around me came
From them I could not run
They took away my coach and six
Then I was quite undone.

My wife so sorrowfully pitied my case
My children round me cried
To think that I in gaol must lie
Until the day I die.

BUTTERCUP JOE

GG/1/3/88, Richard Hall, Itchen Abbas, Hampshire, 1905.

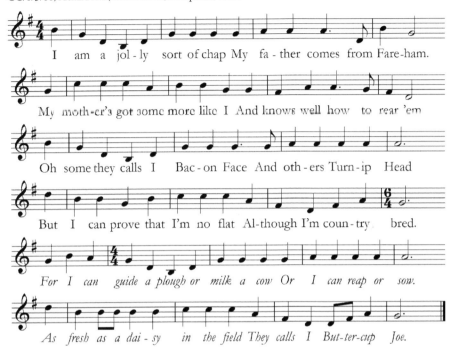

I am a jolly sort of chap
My father comes from Fareham.
My mother's got some more like I
And knows well how to rear 'em.
Oh some they calls I Bacon Face
And others Turnip Head
But I can prove that I'm no flat*
Although I'm country-bred.

Chorus: *For I can guide a plough or milk a
   cow*
Or I can reap or sow
As fresh as a daisy in the field
They calls I Buttercup Joe.

Those nobby swells they laugh and chaff
To see I eat fat bacon
They could not touch that country stuff
But that's where they're mistaken
On wine and grog they do their airs
And lord it at their ease
But give I fat pork from the sty
Or a lump of bread and cheese.

Oh bain't it fine in summertime
When we go out haymaking?
The lasses they will all turn out
And freedom will be taken
They like to get us country chaps
Of course, in harmless play
They like to get us country chaps
And roll us in the hay.

You should just see my young woman
They calls her our Mary
She works as busy as a bee
In Farmer Kellyson's dairy
Oh bain't her suet dumplings good?
By Jove, I mean to try 'em
And ask her if she wouldn't splice
With a rusty chap like I am.

*fool (opposite of sharp)

THE BUXOM LASS (THE MOWER)

Tune: HAM/5/33/51, H. Hooper, Byer, Dorset, February 1907.
Text: HAM/5/33/51; augmented from broadside by Jackson, Birmingham (British Library, LR.271 a.2., vol. 1.1, no. 111).

As I walked out one morning, I met a buxom lass
Belonging to a dairyman, she had a field of grass
And it grew between two mountains at the foot of a running spring
So she hired me to cut it down while the birds did sweetly sing.

I said, My handsome fair maid, what wages do you give?
For mowing is hard labour unless your scythe is good.
She said, If you do please me well, as I am a lady clear
I will give you a crown an acre and plenty of strong beer.

I said, My pretty fair maid, I like your wages well
And if I mow your grass down you shall say it is done well
For my scythe is in good order, it lately has been ground
So, my bonny lass, I'll mow your grass till it's down unto the ground.

She said, My lusty young man, and will you now begin
For my grass is in good order, I long to have it in
And it is such pleasant weather, I long to clear the ground
So keep your scythe in order to mow my meadow down.

With courage like a lion I entered in the field
But before I'd mowed one swathe of grass, oh I was obliged to yield
But before I'd mowed one swathe of grass, my scythe being bent and broke
So she said, My lusty young man, you're tired of your work.

She said, My lusty young man, you're tired of your work
For mowing is hard labour and weakening to the back
For mowing is hard labour and you must it forsake
So around my little meadow you may use your fork and rake.

I said, My handsome fair maid, pray do not on me frown
For if I stop the summer through I cannot cut it down
For it is such a pleasant place and bears such crops of grass
It is well watered by the spring which makes it grow so fast.

CAPTAIN WARD (CAPTAIN WARD AND THE RAINBOW)

Tune: GG/1/5/241, Isaac Hobbes, Micheldever, Hampshire, May 1906.
Text: GG/1/5/241; stanza 2 and first line of stanza 3 from GG/1/10/613, Stephen Phillimore, Andover, Hampshire, August 1906.

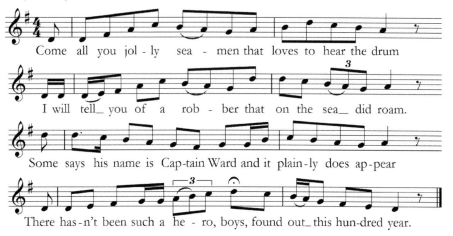

Come all you jolly seamen that loves to hear the drum
I will tell you of a robber that on the sea did roam.
Some says his name is Captain Ward and it plainly does appear
There hasn't been such a hero, boys, found out this hundred year.

Our king he built a galliant ship, a ship of noble fame
She is called the saucy *Rainbow* if you must know her name
Our ship she is well-rigged and fitted out for sea
With eleven hundred seamen to keep her company.

We sailed round and round, my boys, where this great robber lay
Where is the master of your ship? the gallant *Rainbow* cried.
Lo, here am I, says Captain Ward, my name I'll never deny
And if you are one of the king's ships you're welcome to pass by.

If you've any resolution your skill all for to try
You and I will have a battle before we do pass by.
With all my heart, says Captain Ward, I value you not one pin
Although you shows your brass without, I am good steel within.

So at eight o'clock in the morning this battle did begin
And so it did continue till eight o'clock again.
Fight on, fight on, says Captain Ward, your sport well pleases me
And if you fight for a month or more, your master I will be.

I never robbed an English ship nor ship of noble fame
Nor yet the blackguard Dutchman that sail all on the main
Go home, go home and tell your king, and tell him this from me
That if he reigns king over all the land, it's I'll reign king at sea.

CATCH-ME-IF-YOU-CAN

Tune: HAM/5/33/46, Marina Russell, Upwey, Dorset. January/February 1907; bar five embellished as per HAM/4/23/24.
Text: HAM/4/23/24, William Farnham, South Perrot, Dorset, June 1906; opening amended from broadside.

'Twas early, early all in the spring
The small birds they did sweetly sing
So sweetly they were singing
So sweetly they were singing.

As I walked forth down by a riverside
A pretty girl I chanced to spy
She was taking of the air, o
She was taking of the air, o.

I said, Fair maid, will you go along with
me?
I'll show you what you never, never see
I'll show you shady bowers
I'll show you shady bowers.

So this fair maid gave her consent
And along with me she straightway went
And soon he gained her favour
And soon he gained her favour.

So now you've had your will of me
And robbed me of my sweet liberty
Pray tell to me your name, sir
Pray tell to me your name, sir.

My name is Catch-me-if-you-can
And I'll marry you when I return
When I return from the wars, o
When I return from the wars, o.

When six long months were over and past
The fair maid she grew thick round the
waist
And she thought of shady bowers
And she thought of shady bowers.

When nine long months were over and
gone
This young maid bore a beautiful son
But then there was no father
But then there was no father.

So she sent out a horse and man
Go, catch this young man if you can
Go, catch him and no other
Go, catch him and no other.

They catched the rogue and bound him fast
They took this young man in at last
And robbed him of his pleasure
And robbed him of his pleasure.

39

THE CLUSTER OF NUTS

Tune: HAM/2/7/14, William Bartlett, Wimborne Union, Dorset, 1905.
Text: mainly from broadside, without imprint (British Library, 11621.h.11, vol. 8, no. 482).

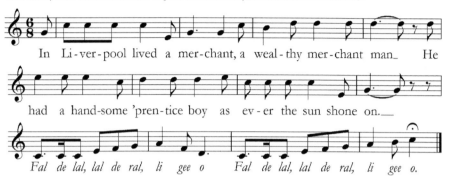

In Liverpool lived a merchant, a wealthy merchant man
He had a handsome 'prentice boy as ever the sun shone on.

Chorus: *Fal de lal, lal de ral, li gee o*
Fal de lal, lal de ral, li gee o.

He was proper tall and handsome, and everything being right
Said he could sleep with a pretty girl and kiss her twelve times a night.

His mistress being standing by and hearing him say so
She said, Jack, I'll lay a wager that you don't perform it so.

Five pounds will be the wager and twelve will be the bet
And I myself will be the judge when we are both in bed.

His master being from home that night and everything being right
He slipped into bed with his mistress and kissed her twelve times that night.

One of them being drowsy which there was no virtue in
Which caused his mistress for to say, The wager I did win.

If I did not win the wager, which I suppose you'd like
I'll leave it to my master when he comes home tonight.

Be off, you saucy fellow, would you have your master know?
Indeed, upon my honour, I do intend it so.

When his master came home that night and at his supper sat
Says Jack unto his master, I'd like you to decide a bet.

As my mistress and I were riding down by the greenwood side
And I upon your mare's back, a cluster of nuts I spied.

I said there were twelve, and she said there was eleven
Then I shoved them into her apron and there were five and seven.

Five and seven is a dozen as I've heard people say
So, Jack, you've won your wager and your mistress must you pay.

His mistress being standing by and hearing him say so
She clinked down the wager and was glad to be let off so.

Now when his master is from home she continually stuffs his guts
And she claps him on the shoulder, saying, Jack, remember the nuts.

THE COUNTRY CARRIER

Tune: GG/1/21/1401, Henry Norris, Farnham Union, Surrey, April 1909.
Text GG/1/2/68, William Randall, Hursley, Hampshire, June 1905.

I am a country carrier, a jovial soul am I
I whistle and sing from morn till night and trouble I defy
I've one to bear me company, of work she does her share
She's not my wife, but upon my life she's a rattling old bay mare.

Chorus: *Then round goes the wheels and troubles I'll defy*
It's jogging along together, my boys, my rattling mare and I.

It's up and down the countryside my mare and I do go
The folks they kindly greet us as we journey to and fro
The children they all cheer and the old ones stop and stare
They lift their eyes with great surprise to Joe and his old bay mare.

Now when the loads are heavy and she's trolling up the hill
I by her side assists her, she works with such good will
She knows I loves her well enough because the whip I spare
I would rather hurt myself than hurt my rattling old bay mare.

Now when the town we reaches she rattles over the stones
She lifts her hoofs so splendidly, she's not one of your lazy drones
Then clear the road for Joseph comes, you crawlers all take care!
With a driver smart and a carrier's cart, it's Joe and his old bay mare.

I would not change my station for the noblest in the land
I would not be prime minister or anything so grand
I would not be an alderman to live in luxury
There's not an estate would separate my rattling mare and I.

THE CRAFTY MAID'S POLICY

Tune: HAM/5/32/23, Marina Russell, Upwey, Dorset, January/February 1907.
Text: HAM/5/32/23; augmented from broadside by Disley, London (British Library, 11621.h.11, vol. 8, no. 500).

Come listen awhile and I'll sing you a song
Of three merry gentlemen riding along.
They met a fair maid and one to her did say
I'm afraid this cold morning will do you some harm.

Oh no, kind sir, said the maid, you're mistaken
To think this cold morn will do me some harm
There's one thing I crave that lies 'twixt your legs
If you give me that it will keep me warm.

Then since you crave it, my dear, you shall have it
If you'll go with me to yonder green tree
Then since you crave it, my dear, you shall have it
And I'll make these gentlemen witness to be.

Then the gentleman alighted and straightway she mounted
And looking the gentleman hard in the face
Saying, You knew not my meaning, you wrong understood me
And away she went galloping down the long lane.

Oh gentlemen, lend me one of your horses
That I may ride after her down the long lane
If I overtake her, I'll warrant I'll make her
Return unto me my own horse again.

Soon as this fair maid she saw him a-coming
She instantly then took a pistol in hand
Saying, Doubt not my skill that you I might kill
I would have you stand back or you are a dead man.

Oh why do you spend your time here in talking?
Oh why do you spend your time here in vain?
Come, give her a guinea, 'tis what she deserves
I'll warrant she'll give you your horse back again.

Oh no, kind sir, you are vastly mistaken
If it's his loss, then it is my gain
For you are witness that he gave it to me
And away she went galloping over the plain.

CREEPING JANE

Tune: HAM/4/21/17, Sam Dawe, Beaminster, Dorset, June 1906.
Text: HAM/4/21/17; slightly augmented from a broadside by H. Such, London.

I'll sing you a song and a very pretty song
It's concerning of Creeping Jane
Oh she never saw a horse nor a gelding in her life
That she vallied* not the half of a pin
Fal the dee, fal the dal the di do
That she vallied not the half of a pin, fal the dee.

When Creeping Jane came to the starting post
The gentlemen viewed her all around
And all they had to say concerning Creeping Jane
She's not able to gallop o'er the ground
Fal the dee, fal the dal the di do
She's not able to gallop o'er the ground, fal the dee.

When Creeping Jane she came to the first mile post
Creeping Jane was far behind
Oh the rider put the whip round little Jenny's neck
And he says, My little lady, never mind
Fal the dee, etc.

When Creeping Jane she came to the second mile post
Creeping Jane she kept lingering behind
Oh the rider put the spurs into little Jenny's waist
And he says, My little lady, never mind
Fal the dee, etc.

When Creeping Jane she came to the third mile post
Creeping Jane she looked fresh and smart
Oh the rider put a posy into little Jenny's ear
And she passed them all like a dart
Fal the dee, etc.

Now Creeping Jane she've a-won that race
And she scarcely sweat one drop
She is able for to gallop o'er the same ground again
While the others are not able for to trot
Fal the dee, etc.

Now Creeping Jane she's dead and gone
And her body lies under cold ground
I will send to her master one favour for to beg
For to keep her little body from the hounds
Fal the dee, etc.

*valued

THE CRUEL SHIP'S CARPENTER

Tune: GG/1/11/698, Alfred Stride, Dibden, Hampshire, June 1907.
Text: GG/1/12/712, George Baldwin, Tichborne, Hampshire, June 1907.

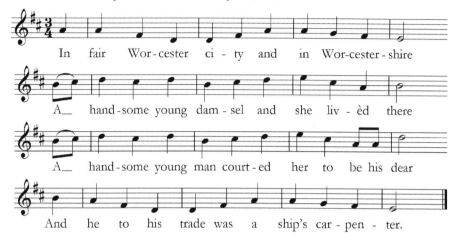

In fair Worcester city and in Worcestershire
A handsome young damsel and she lived there
A handsome young man courted her to be his dear
And he to his trade was a ship's carpenter.

Now the king wanted seamen to go on the sea
Which caused this young damsel to sigh and to say
O William, O William, don't you go to sea
Remember the vows that you made unto me.

It was early next morning before it was day
He went to his Polly, these words he did say
O Polly, o Polly, you must go with me
Before we are married my friends for to see.

He led her through groves and valleys so deep
Which caused this young damsel to sigh and to weep
O William, o William, you have led me astray
On purpose my innocent life to betray.

It is true, it is true, these words he did say
For all the long night I've been digging your grave.
The grave it being open, the spade standing by
Which caused this young damsel to sigh and to cry.

O William, o William, oh pardon my life
I never will covet to be your sweet wife
I will travel the country to set you quite free
Oh pardon, oh pardon my baby and me.

No pardon I'll give thee, no time for to stand
And with that he had a sharp knife in his hand
He stabbed her heart through till the blood it did flow
Then into the grave her fair body did throw.

He covered it up so safe and secure
A-thinking no one should find it he was very sure
Then he went on board to sail the world round
Before that the murder should ever be found.

It was early next morning before it was day
Our captain came up, these words he did say
There's a murder on board and it's lately been done
Our ship she's in mourning and cannot sail on.

Then up stepped one, Indeed it's not me.
Then up stepped another, the same he did say.
Then up stepped young William to stamp and to swear
Indeed it's not me, sir, I vow and declare.

As he was returning from the captain with speed
He met his own Polly which made his heart bleed
She ripped him, she stripped him, she tore him in three
Saying, William, remember my baby and me.

THE CUCKOO

Tune: HAM/2/2/5, Mrs Gulliver, Combe Florey, Somerset, 1905.
Text: HAM/2/2/5; stanzas 5 and 6 augmented from a version noted by Alfred Williams from Alice Barnett,
Quenington, Gloucestershire (Alfred Williams MS Collection, Gl 127).

The cuck-oo is a fine bird, he sings as he flies
He brings us good tid-ings and tells us no lies
He_ sucks the sweet flow-ers for to make his voice clear
And the more he cries cuck-oo, the_ sum-mer draws near.

The cuckoo is a fine bird, he sings as he flies
He brings us good tidings and tells us no lies
He sucks the sweet flowers for to make his voice clear
And the more he cries cuckoo, the summer draws near.

'Twas walking and talking and walking was I
For to meet my true-lover, he's coming by and by
For to meet it's a pleasure, and to part it's a grief
And a false-hearted young man is worse than a thief.

For a thief he will rob you of all that you have
But a false-hearted young man will bring you to your grave
For the grave it will rot you and bring you to dust
So a false-hearted young man I'll never more trust.

Oh once I had a colour like the bud of a rose
But now I'm so pale as the lily that grows
A flower in the morning cut down in full bloom
What do you think I am coming to by the loving of one?

Come all pretty maidens wherever you be
Don't trust in young soldiers in any degree
They will kiss you and court you, poor girls to deceive
There's not one in twenty a maid can believe.

They will laugh under their hat, love, as they see you pass by
They'll bow with their body and wink with one eye
They will kiss you and court you and swear to be true
But the very next moment they'll bid you adieu.

THE DANDY HUSBAND

Tune: GG/1/8/452, George Smith, Fareham, Hampshire, July 1906.
Text: first half of stanza 1, second half of stanza 8, and chorus from GG/1/8/452; remainder from a broadside by
Fortey, London, slightly abbreviated (British Library, 11621.h.11, vol. 7, no. 335, with ten stanzas and chorus).

When I was twenty years of age a-courting I did go
Unto some dandy barber's clerk who has filled my heart with woe
He has caused me for to rue the day that I was made his wife
He cannot do right by day or night, it's true upon my life.

Chorus: *So women all take my advice and mark what I do say*
If you should wed a dandy man, you will ever rue the day.

Now every night when he's in bed like an elephant he lays
He never pulls his breeches off and he sleeps in women's stays
His mouth is like a turnpike gate, his nose in length a yard and a half
And if you saw his handsome legs I'm sure they'd make you laugh.

It was upon last Christmas Day, as true as I'm a sinner
My dandy husband swore he would stay home and cook the dinner
He took the plums and flour and he mixed them in his hat
Then in the pot upon the lot, the rogue, he boiled some fat.

Last Sunday morning he got home all by his own desire
My leghorn bonnet and my cap he took to light the fire
He took the tea things from the shelf for to clean off the dirt
He washed them in the chamber pot and wiped them with his shirt.

One day when I was very ill, he went to buy a fowl
He bought a pair, I don't know where, a magpie and an owl
He put them in a pot to boil tied in a dirty cloth
He boiled them both all feathers and guts and said it was famous broth.

I thought an apple pudding for dinner I would have
And as he stayed at home that day, to cook it he did crave
He tied it in a coal bag with a nasty, dirty rope
And in it mixed my blue bag and near a pound of soap.

As we was walking up the street, 'twas arm in arm together
It very fast began to snow, he said, What rainy weather!
And if he saw a hackney coach he would swear it was a gig
He could not tell, I do declare, a donkey from a pig.

Now you may talk of dandy wives but tell me if you can
Is there a woman in the world can match a dandy man?
If I was married to a sweep, oh how I'd bless the day
If I could see my dandy man sent off to Botany Bay.

THE DARLING BOY

Tune: HAM/2/1/24, Mrs Gulliver, Combe Florey, Somerset, April/May 1905.
Text: HAM/2/1/24; stanza 5 from an unspecified broadside.

I wish I had never seen no man at all
Since love's been a grief and has proved my downfall
Since love's been a grief and a tyrant to me
I lost my love fighting for sweet liberty.

I wish I had never seen his curly hair
Nor yet had I been in his company there
With his red rosy cheeks and his rolling dark eye
And his flattering tongue caused my poor heart to sigh.

Some people come to me and thus they do say
Your love he is 'listed and gone far away
But if ever he return I will crown him with joy
And I'll cross the sweet lips of my own darling boy.

If I'd wings like a linnet, oh where would I fly?
I would fly to the arms of my dear darling boy
Then in his soft bosom I'd build up my nest
And I'd lay my head down on his soft snowy breast.

Some say I'm with child, but that I'll deny
Some say I'm with child but I'll prove it a lie
I'll tarry a while and soon let them know
That he likes me too well to serve me so.

Oh some do wear 'spensions but I do wear none
And they that don't love me can leave me alone
They can have me or leave me, or else let me go
For I don't give a straw if they have me or no.

THE DEATH OF PARKER

Tune: GG/1/2/15, Mr W. Rundle, landlord of the Farmer's Inn, St Merryn, Cornwall, May 1905.
Text: GG/1/2/15; first two lines of stanza 2 from GG/1/11/666, unknown singer at Hannington Kingsclere, Hampshire, May 1907; a few alterations from GG/1/17/1109, Mrs Barnes, Medstead, Alton, Hampshire, December 1907.

Ye gods above, protect the widow and with pity look down on me
Help me, help me out of trouble and through this sad calamity.
Parker was a wild young sailor, fortune to him did prove unkind
Although he was hanged up for mutiny, worse than him was left behind.

Chorus: *Farewell, Parker, thou bright angel, once thou wast old England's pride*
Although he was hanged up for mutiny, worse than him was left behind.

Young Parker was my lawful husband, my bosom friend whom I loved so dear
Though doomed by law he was to suffer, I was not allowed to come near
At length I saw the yellow flag flying, the signal for my true-love to die
The gun was fired which was required to hang him all on the yardarm so high.

The boatman did his best endeavour to reach the shore without delay
And there I stood waiting just like a mermaid to carry the corpse of my husband away
In the dead of night when all was silent and thousands of people lay fast asleep
Me and my poor maidens beside me into the burying ground did creep.

With trembling hands instead of shovels the mould from his coffin we scratched away
Until we came to the corpse of Parker and carried him off without delay
A mourning coach stood there a-waiting and off to London we drove with speed
And there we had him most decently buried and a sermon preached over him indeed.

Down by the Woods and Shady Green Trees (The Shady Green Tree)

HAM/4/30/1, Mrs Bowen, Dorchester Union, Dorset, December 1906.

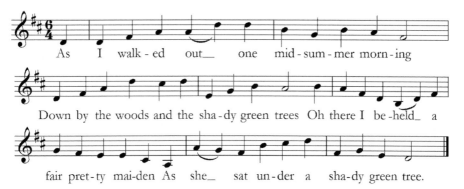

As I walk-ed out__ one mid-sum-mer morn-ing
Down by the woods and the sha-dy green trees Oh there I be-held__ a
fair pret-ty mai-den As she__ sat un-der a sha-dy green tree.

As I walked out one midsummer morning
Down by the woods and the shady green
     trees
Oh there I beheld a fair pretty maiden
As she sat under a shady green tree.

I stepped up to her and said, My dear jewel
You are the first girl that ever won me
You never shall want for gold nor for silver
If you will place your affections on me.

She said, Young man, you are better
     deserving
For I am a poor girl of low degree
Besides, your friends will always be
     grumbling
So in my low station contented I'll be.

Don't talk of friends nor yet of relations
For they have no portion at all to give me
For I am a young man and you are a virgin
Married unto you tomorrow I'll be.

She sat herself down and I sat myself by her
Then I began for to rifle her charms
With sweet melting kisses and many fond
     embraces
We fell asleep in each other's arms.

We had not been there passing three hours
Down by the woods and the shady green
     trees
Before I awoke and found her no virgin.
Married unto you I never will be.

She said, Young man, you've been my
     undoer
And how can you so cruelly prove?
And how can I pass any more as a virgin
Since you have had your will of me?

Come all pretty girls, by me take warning
Don't trust a young man in any degree
For when they've enjoyed the fruits of your
     garden
They will go and leave you as he have left
     me.

THE DROWNED LOVER (THE LOVER'S LAMENT FOR HER SAILOR)

GG/1/8/474, James Lake, Dummer, Hampshire, August 1906.

As I was a-walking down by the seashore
Where the winds and the waves and the billows did roar
I heard a shrill voice make a sorrowful sound
'Midst the winds and the waves and the waters all round.

Chorus: *Crying, Oh my love's gone, he's the lad I adore*
He's gone and I never, no, never, shall see my love more.

She was dressed like some goddess, she looked like some queen
She's the fairest of women that my eyes e'er had seen
I told her I'd marry her myself if she pleased
But the answer she gave was, My love's on the seas.

I never will marry nor be no man's bride
For I mean to live single all the days of my life
It's the loss of my sailor I deeply deplore
He's lost in the seas, I shan't see him no more.

The shells of the ocean shall be my last bed
And the fish of the seas shall swim over my head.
She plunged her fair body right into the deep
And closed her fair eyes in the waters to sleep.

FAREWELL, DEAREST NANCY

HAM/4/31/20, Marina Russell, Upwey, Dorset, January/February 1907.

Fare - well, dear - est Nan - cy, oh now I must leave you
Un - to the West In - dies my course I must steer
I know ve - ry well that my ab - sence will grieve you
But, my dear, I will_ re - turn in the spring_ of the year.

Farewell, dearest Nancy, oh now I must leave you
Unto the West Indies my course I must steer
I know very well that my absence will grieve you
But, my dear, I will return in the spring of the year.

Oh don't talk of going, my dearest jewel
Don't talk of leaving me here on the shore
It's your sweet company that I do admire
Therefore I shall die if I never see you more.

Don't let my long voyage be a trouble unto you
Don't let my long absence run sore in your mind
Although we are parted, my dear, I'm true-hearted
And we will be married when I do return.

Just like some little sea-boy, my dear, I'll go with you
In the midst of all dangers, oh I'll be your friend
And when that the cold stormy winds are a-blowing
Then, my dear, I shall be with you to wait on you then.

Your lily-white hands cannot handle a cable
Nor your pretty little feet to the topmast can't go
Nor the cold stormy weather, my dear, you can't endure
Therefore to the seas, dearest Nancy, don't go.

As she stood a-wailing the ship set a-sailing
Tears down her cherry cheeks like torrents did flow
And her lily-white hands in sorrow stood a-wringing
Crying, O my dearest jewel, I shall never see you more.

FATHOM THE BOWL

GG/1/10/587, Henry Adams, Basingstoke, Hampshire, September 1906.

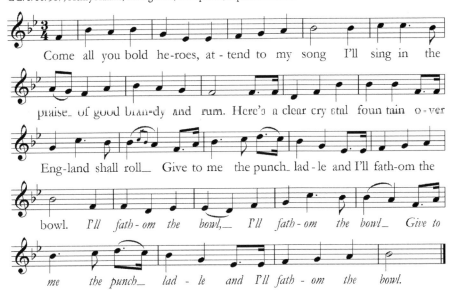

Come all you bold heroes, attend to my song
I'll sing in the praise of good brandy and rum.
Here's a clear crystal fountain over England shall roll
Give to me the punch ladle and I'll fathom the bowl.

Chorus: *I'll fathom the bowl, I'll fathom the bowl*
Give to me the punch ladle and I'll fathom the bowl.

From France we get brandy, from Jamaica comes rum
Sweet oranges and lemons from Portugal come
Strong beer and good cider in England is sold
Give to me the punch ladle and I'll fathom the bowl.

My wife she's a tyrant, she sits at her ease
She scolds and she grumbles, she does as she please
She may scold, she may grumble till she's black as a coal
Give to me the punch ladle and I'll fathom the bowl.

My father he lies in the depth of the sea
Cold rocks for a pillow, what matter to he?
Here's a clear crystal fountain over England shall roll
Give to me the punch ladle and I'll fathom the bowl.

THE FEMALE DRUMMER

Tune: GG/1/17/1081, William Bone, Alton, Hampshire, November 1907.
Text: GG/1/17/1081; second half of stanza 3 altered to conform with current traditional versions; and some adjustment to stanza order.

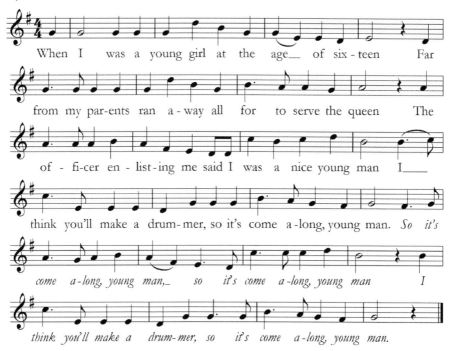

When I was a young girl at the age of sixteen
Far from my parents ran away all for to serve the queen
The officer enlisting me said I was a nice young man
I think you'll make a drummer, so it's come along, young man
So it's come along, young man, so it's come along, young man
I think you'll make a drummer, so it's come along, young man.

I was sent up to my quarters all for to go to bed
And sleeping by a soldier's side I did not feel afraid
In pulling off my red jacket it often made me smile
To think I was a drummer and a maiden all the while
And a maiden all the while, and a maiden all the while
To think I was a drummer and a maiden all the while.

My waist being long and slender, my fingers thin and small
All for to beat upon the drum I soon exceeded all
I played upon my kettledrums like other drummers played
I played upon my kettledrums and still remained a maid
And still remained a maid, and still remained a maid
I played upon my kettledrums and still remained a maid.

I was sent up to London all for to guard the Tower
And there I might have been till this very day and hour
But a young girl fell in love with me, I told her I was a maid
And straightway to my officer the secret she betrayed
The secret she betrayed, the secret she betrayed
And straightway to my officer the secret she betrayed.

The officer he sent for me to know if it was true
Of such a thing I cannot nor I won't believe of you.
He looked me in the face and he smiled as he said
It's a pity we should lose you, such a drummer as you made
Such a drummer as you made, such a drummer as you made
It's a pity we should lose you, such a drummer as you made.

So fare you well, dear officer, you have been kind to me
And likewise, dear comrades, I'm not forgetting thee
And if your army should be short for the want of any man
I'll put on my hat and feather and I'll march with you again
I'll march with you again, I'll march with you again
I'll put on my hat and feather and I'll march with you again. *

* *more usually And I'll beat the drum again*

THE FEMALE HIGHWAYMAN

Tune: HAM/4/25/17, Mrs Young, Long Barton, Dorset, July 1906.
Text: HAM/4/25/17; stanzas 6 and 7 from HAM/3/18/3, Mrs Crawford, West Milton, Dorset, May 1906; stanza 2 improved from broadside.

Shil - lo, Shil-lo, one day,— one day She dressed her - self in man's— ar- ray. With a sword and pis - tol hung by her side To meet her true love To meet her true love a - way she ride.

Shillo,* Shillo, one day, one day
She dressed herself in man's array
With a sword and pistol hung by her side
To meet her true-love
To meet her true-love away she ride.

As she was riding over the plain
She met her true-love and bid him stand
Stand and deliver, kind sir, she said
Or else this moment
Or else this moment I will shoot you dead.

Oh when she'd robbed him of his store
She said, Kind sir, there is one thing more
A diamond ring which I know you have
Deliver it
Deliver it your life to save.

My diamond ring a token is
My life I'll lose, the ring I'll save.
Being tender-hearted much like a dove
She rode away
She rode away from her true-love.

Next morning in the garden green
Just like two lovers they were seen
He saw his watch hanging by her clothes
Which made him blush
Which made him blush like any rose.

What makes you blush, you silly thing?
I thought to have had your diamond ring
'Tis I that robbed you on the plain
So here's your gold, love
So here's your gold, love, and watch again.

I did intend and 'twas to know
Whether you was my true-love or no
So now I have a contented mind
My heart and all
My heart and all, my dear, are thine.

Oh then this couple married were
And they did live a happy pair
The bells did ring and the music play
And they've got pleasure
And they've got pleasure both night and
    day.

broadsides give the heroine's name as Sylvie

FLASH COMPANY

GG/1/7/365, Job Read, Southampton, July 1906.

First I loved William and then I loved John
But now I love Thomas, he's a clever young man.
With his white cotton stockings and his high ankled shoes
He wears a velvet jacket, like a flash lad he goes.

It's fiddling and dancing was all his delight
And keeping flash company has ruined him quite
Has ruined him quite and a great many more
If he hadn't kept flash company he had never been so poor.

Oh take this yellow handkerchief in remembrance of me
And wear it all round your neck when in flash company
Dry up your briny tears and don't look so sad
There's plenty more flash girls all wish to be had.

Singers frequently end this song with one of these 'floaters' concerning constant – or even unconstant – love, such as:

Oh once I had a colour as red as a rose
But now I'm pale as the lily that grows
Like a flower in the garden all my colour is gone
You see what I've come to through doing what I've done.

The rocks shall run to water and the sea shall run dry
If ever I prove false to the girl that loves I
In the middle of the ocean there shall grow a myrtle tree
If ever I prove false to the girl that loves me.

THE FROLIC (THE SAILOR'S FROLIC)

Tune is a mixture of HAM/3/17/17, J. Greening, North Bridport, Dorset, 1906 and HAM/2/7/26, William Bartlett, Wimborne Union, Dorset, 1905.
Text: HAM/2/7/26; first half of stanza 2, second half of stanza 4, first half of stanza 6, and first half of stanza 8 added from a broadside.

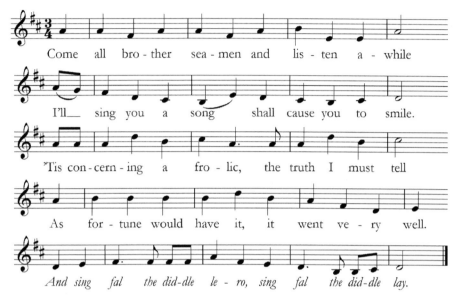

Come all brother seamen and listen awhile
I'll sing you a song shall cause you to smile
'Tis concerning a frolic, the truth I must tell
As fortune would have it, it went very well.

Chorus: *And sing fal the diddle lero, sing fal the diddle lay.*

I needing a drink to an alehouse went in
To dance and to caper I soon did begin.
Young doxies were there by one, two, and three
Thinks I to myself, one of them is for me.

One of them being well-rigged in a new black silk gown
I tipped her the wink and she came by me and sit down
Then I called to the waiter to bring me some gin
She said, My dear jewel, and that's just the thing.

And now for my Jack I will lodging provide
For I am the girl that do lie by your side.
Fifteen and sixpence, the waiter did say
I paid down my money, went upstairs straightway.

So I quickly unrigged and I jumped into bed
And my money I planted safe under my head.
When doxy and I wished each t'other good night
I shammed fast asleep and she thought herself right.

In a little while after young doxy arose
And searched the room round for to find out my clothes
She searched the room round for 'twas all her design
To discover the place where I kept all my coin.

Now I had a stick by me the size of my thumb
I jumped out of bed and I well laid it on
I stepped round the room after, I followed my blows
I gave her no time for to slip on her clothes.

In the morning I looked to see what I could find
For madam in her haste had left all things behind
When I looked in the pockets of her gown and her coat
I found nine golden sovereigns and two five-pound notes.

THE GAY PLOUGHBOY

HAM/4/27/8, Charles Whiffen, Sandford, Dorset, November 1906.

Come all my pretty ploughboys and listen to my song
One story I will tell you that do to love belong
How I do rise so early and do tend my team with joy
And I boldly do my duty like a gay ploughboy
Like a gay ploughboy
And I boldly do my duty like a gay ploughboy.

It's of a youthful damsel who lived in a grove
Whose mind did seem contented with rural peace and love
Down in her father's garden she singed songs of joy
Her melody was praising of her gay ploughboy
Of her gay ploughboy, etc.

Says the mother to the daughter, You seem to love him well
It seems as if your tender heart all in his breast doth dwell
The lads they are so rakish, young maidens to decoy
So you may see upon your knee a little ploughboy
A little ploughboy, etc.

Oh, then replied young Patty, he's just the lad for me
With him I can live happy, contented, gay and free
He do arise so early and tend his team with joy
And none can be so happy as the gay ploughboy
As the gay ploughboy, etc.

Young William with his horses returning home from plough
He showed the maid a ring of gold, her tongue could not say no
He said, My pretty Patty, the parson we'll employ
And none will be so happy as the gay ploughboy
As the gay ploughboy, etc.

So now they are united, young William goes to plough
And she arise delighted to milk her spotted cow
Down in a rural cottage where none can them annoy
Young Patty she lives happy with her gay ploughboy
With her gay ploughboy, etc.

GEORGE COLLINS

Tune: GG/1/19/1193, Henry Blake, Bartley, Hampshire, September 1908.
Text: collation of GG/1/11/658, George Hiscock, Minstead, Hampshire, November 1906; GG/1/6/327,
George Blake, Southampton, Hampshire, 17 July 1906; GG/1/7/419; Henry Stansbridge, Lyndhurst,
Hampshire, 27 September 1906 (son-in-law of George Blake); GG/1/8/439, Phillip Gaylor, Minstead,
Hampshire, 27 September 1906; and GG/1/19/1193.

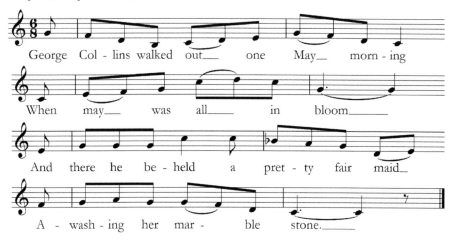

George Collins walked out one May morning
When may was all in bloom
And there he beheld a pretty fair maid
A-washing her marble stone.

She whooped, she holloed, she highered her voice
And held up her lily-white hand
Come hither to me, George Collins, she said
And thy life shall not last thee long.

George Collins stepped up to the fair waterside
And over the water sprang he
He clasped his arms round her middle so small
And kissed her red rosy cheeks.

George Collins went home to his own father's gate
And so loudly he did ring
And who should come down but his own father dear
To let George Collins in.

Arise, my dear father, and let me in
Arise, dear mother, and make my bed
Arise, my dear sister, and get me a napkin
A napkin to bind round my head.

And if I should chance to die this night
As I suppose I shall
Bury me under that marble stone
That's against fair Helen's wall.

Fair Helen sits in her room so fine
A-working her silken skein
Then she saw the finest corpse a-coming
That ever the sun shone on.

She said unto her Irish maid
Whose corpse is this so fine?
It is George Collins's corpse a-coming
That once was a true-lover of thine.

You go upstairs and fetch me the sheet
That's wove with a silver twine
And hang it over George Collins's corpse
Tomorrow it shall hang over mine.

Come put him down, my six pretty lads
And open his coffin so fine
That I might kiss his lily-white lips
For ten thousand times he has kissed mine.

The news was carried to fair London town
And wrote all on fair London's gate
That six pretty maidens died all of one night
And all for George Collins's sake.

THE GREEN BED

Tune: GG/1/20/1222, James Buckland, Micheldever, Hampshire, November 1908.
Text: GG/1/11/639, Benjamin Arnold, Easton, Hampshire, November 1906; augmented from a broadside.

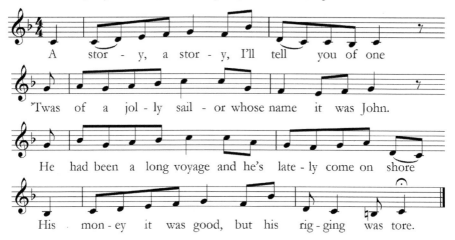

A story, a story, I'll tell you of one
'Twas of a jolly sailor whose name it was John
He had been a long voyage and he's lately come on shore
His money it was good, but his rigging was tore.

He appeared in my eyes like one very poor
He came to the house where he had lodged in before
You're welcome in, young Johnny, you're welcome from the sea
For last night my daughter Molly was dreaming of thee.

What sort of voyage, dear Johnny, have you made?
What sort of voyage? this old bawd she said.
It's a very poor voyage, our ship and cargo lost
And on the wide ocean so greatly I've been tossed.

Where is your daughter Molly? Come fetch her down to me
Call your daughter Molly and sit her on my knee.
No, my daughter's busy, John, and cannot come to you
Nor neither will I trust you for one pot or two.

Johnny being tired, he hung down his head
He called for a candle to light him up to bed.
Our beds are all engaged, John, and have been for a week
And for a fresh lodging poor Jack he must seek.

What money do I owe you? young Johnny he did say
What money do I owe you? Come, tell to me I pray.
Here's four and forty shillings, John, you owe me of old.
Then out of his pocket he pulled handfuls of gold.

At the sight of the gold the landlady did rue
At the jingling of the money, downstairs young Molly flew
She huddled him, she cuddled him, she called him her dear
Saying, The green bed is empty, young Johnny might sleep there.

Oh sooner than I'd lie in your green bed, I know
I would rather lie out in the cold and the snow
If I hadn't got no money, out of doors I'd be turned
So it's you and your old mother might go and be burned.

Come all you young sailors that sails on the main
That do get your living in cold storms of rain
And when you have a-got it, pray lay it up in store
For the fear that your companions should turn you out of doors.

THE GREEN MOSSY BANKS OF THE LEA

GG/1/2/49, John Carter, Twyford, Hampshire, June 1905.

When___ first in this coun-try a stran-ger,___
cur-i-o-si-ty caused me to roam___
O'er___ Eur-ope I res-olved to be a ran-ger___
when I left Phil-a-del-phi-a my home.___
I quick-ly sailed o-ver to Eng - land
where the___ forms of great beau-ty do shine
And at length I be-held a fair dam-sel___
and I wished in my heart she was mine.___

When first in this country a stranger, curiosity caused me to roam
O'er Europe I resolved to be a ranger when I left Philadelphia my home
I quickly sailed over to England where the forms of great beauty do shine
And at length I beheld a fair damsel and I wished in my heart she was mine.

One morning I carelessly rambled where the pure winds and soft breezes do blow
It was down by a clear crystal river where the sweet purling waters did flow
'Twas there I espied a fair creature, some goddess appearing to be
As she rose from the reeds by the water on the green mossy banks of the Lea.

So I stepped up and wished her good morning and her fair cheeks they blushed like a rose
Says I, The green meadows are charming, your guardian I'll be if you choose.
She said, sir, I don't want any guardian, young man, you're a stranger to me
And yonder my father's a-coming o'er the green mossy banks of the Lea.

So I waited till up came her father and cheered up my spirits once more
And I said, Is this your fair daughter, this beautiful girl I adore?
Ten thousand a year is my fortune and a lady your daughter shall be
She shall ride with her chariots and horses o'er the green mossy banks of the Lea.

Then they welcomed me down to their cottage, soon after in wedlock to join
And there I erected a castle in grandeur and splendour to shine
So now the American stranger all pleasures and pastimes can see
With adorable, gentle Matilda on the green mossy banks of the Lea.

So it's all pretty maids pay attention, no matter how poor you may be
For there's many a poor girl as handsome as those with a large property
By flattery let no one deceive you whatever your fortune may be
Only look at young, gentle Matilda on the green mossy banks of the Lea.

HAYMAKING COURTSHIP

Tune: GG/1/18/1152, William Hill, Catherington Workhouse, Hampshire, August 1908.
Text: GG/1/18/1152; stanza 5 from GG/1/8/451, George Smith, Fareham, Hampshire, July 1906; stanza 2, line 6, and stanza 7, line 1, from GG/1/17/1091, William Bone, Medstead, Hampshire, November 1907.

A sail-or walk - ing through the fields To see what plea - sure he could
find And there he spied a maid all___ in the shade As she was a
rak - ing As she was a rak - ing All round her mast-er's hay.

A sailor walking through the fields
To see what pleasure he could find
And there he spied a maid all in the shade
As she was a-raking
As she was a-raking
All round her master's hay.

So he boldly stepped up to her
These words to her he then did say
Throw your rake one side and put on your
  gown
And go with your sailor
And go with your sailor
And leave your master's hay.

Suppose my master he should know
That I along with you do go
He would stop my wages, give me no pay
He would stop my wages
He would stop my wages
And turn me right away.

It's kisses sweet and words so kind
Until this fair maid changed her mind
She threw her rake one side and put on her
  gown
And went with the sailor
And went with the sailor
And left her master's hay.

The sailor took her to yonder wake
And treated her with wine and cake
And he gave her rings, ribbons, and gloves
Until he gained her
Until he gained her
Until he gained her love.

Now nine long months were gone and past
Oh this young maid she fell sick at last
Then she cursed the hour, likewise the day
She went with the sailor
She went with the sailor
And left her master's hay.

Now two long years were gone and past
This young sailor returned at last.
Then he married her, made no more delay
Then she blessed the hour
Then she blessed the hour
That she left her master's hay.

THE HERRING SONG

Tune: GG/1/4/155, George Hatherill, Bath, Somerset
Text: HAM/3/12/7, George Hatherill, Bath, Somerset, January 1906.

What did you do with your red herring's
  head?
I made the finest baker that ever baked
  bread.
Bread, oven, and ev'ry fine thing
I think I done well with my jolly herring.

Chorus: *Well, why hasn't told us so?*
So I did long ago
Well, well, well, everything
I think I done well with my jolly herring.

What did you do with your red herring's
  eyes?
I made the finest baker that ever baked pies
Pies, oven, and every fine thing
I think I done well with my jolly herring.

What did you do with your red herring's
  gills?
I made the finest doctor that ever made pills
Pills, doctor, and every fine thing
I think I done well with my jolly herring.

What did you do with your red herring's
  guts?
I made forty-five ladies and fifty-five sluts
Sluts, ladies, and every fine thing
I think I done well with my jolly herring.

What did you do with your red herring's
  skin?
I made so fine a silk dress as ever a lady
  dressed in
Dress, lady, and every fine thing
I think I done well with my jolly herring.

What did you do with your red herring's
  backbone?
I made so fine a mason as ever laid a stone
Stone, mason, and every fine thing
I think I done well with my jolly herring.

What did you do with your red herring's
  tail?
I made the finest ship as ever set sail
Ship, rigging, and every fine thing
I think I done well with my jolly herring.

THE HOSTESS'S DAUGHTER

Tune: HAM/4/23/20, Ishmael Cornick, Burstock, Dorset, June 1906.
Text: adapted from HAM/4/23/20; additions and amendments from HAM/2/2/18, Mrs Gulliver, Combe
Florey, Somerset, 1905.

When first to London town I came
I took my lodging all at some inn
For full five months I did remain
But being a stranger, I fell in danger
By doing so, by doing so.

The landlord had one daughter dear
She was a beauty I do declare
But above her garters I dare not go
But being a stranger, etc.

Her ruby lips, her eyes so blue
Which caused me to love her true
I kissed her rosy lips and cheeks
But being a stranger, etc.

The more I kissed her, this girl being
  young
Her eyes did glisten like the rising sun
In yonder grove I sowed my seed
But being a stranger, etc.

The seeds of love they grew apace
The tears were ever on her face
All for to reap it I could not stay
For being a stranger, I fell in danger

Now when this pretty little babe is born
Oh she must keep it, it is her own
And reap the seeds which I have sown
But being a stranger, I fell in danger
By doing so, by doing so.

I AM A BRISK YOUNG SAILOR

Tune: GG/1/3/87, Richard Hall, Itchen Abbas, Hampshire, 1905.
Text: GG/1/3/87; final eight lines from GG/1/9/542, David Marlow, Basingstoke, Hampshire, August 1906;
first two lines from GG/1/18/1121, William Garratt, Petersfield Workhouse, Hampshire, August 1908.

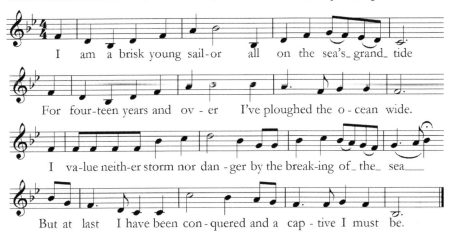

I am a brisk young sail-or all on the sea's grand tide
For four-teen years and ov - er I've ploughed the o - cean wide.
I va-lue neith-er storm nor dan -ger by the break-ing of the sea
But at last I have been con - quered and a cap - tive I must be.

I am a brisk young sailor all on the sea's
grand tide
For fourteen years and over I've ploughed
the ocean wide
I value neither storm nor danger by the
breaking of the sea
But at last I have been conquered and a
captive I must be.

Our ship she's on the ocean and likewise in
full sail
From Linstown* up to London with a
sweet and pleasant gale
And if providence go with us and fortune
do prove kind
I'll be back again in Linstown in fifteen
days' fair wind.

And when we gets to Linstown at the
Putney** we will dine
And there I'll toss a bumper of brandy, ale,
and wine
I would free-like spend ten guineas and
down it should be paid
If I could enjoy young Jeannie, that
handsome chambermaid.

I can't think what's come to me that I
should love a child
I can't think what's come to me that I
should be beguiled
If I was but ten years younger and she as
old as me
I would make myself more bolder and
speak my mind more free.

Now since I cannot marry the girl that I
adore
I'll go and plough the ocean and never
come on shore
I'll journey to some country where no one
do me know
Then perhaps my mind may alter, I wish it
might be so.

(to the second half of the tune)
For I never can find comfort when I at
home do dwell
So, you countrymen and maidens, I wish
you all farewell.

* *the name of the port is given thus in nearly
all versions*
** *in other versions, the Bungay or the Park
Gate*

I'ZE YORKSHIRE, THOUGH IN LUNNON (THE YORKSHIREMAN IN LONDON)

Tune: HAM/4/31/9, J Randall, Broadwey, Dorset, February 1907.
Text: from *The Merry Minstrel* published by Swindells of Manchester (British Library, 1077.d.67.(8.)).

When first to London I arrived
On a visit, on a visit
When first to London I arrived
'Midst heavy rain and thunder
I spied a bonny lass in green
The nicest lass I e'er had seen
I oft heard tell of beauty's queen
Dash me, thinks I, I've found her.

Chorus: *Rite fal the dal the di-gee o
Rite fal the dal lal the lido.*

She blushed and smiled, and smiled and
    blushed
Else 'twas fancy, else 'twas fancy
She blushed and smiled, and smiled and
    blushed
And I looked very simple
Her cheeks were like the new-blown rose
Which on the hedge neglected grows
Her eyes were black as any sloes
And near her mouth a dimple.

She stood stock still, I did the same
Gazing on her, gazing on her
She stood stock still, I did the same
Thinks I, I've made a blunder
Just then her lips turned deathly pale
I says, My love, what do you ail?
Then she told me a dismal tale
How she was scared wi' thunder.

Madam, says I, and made a bow
Scraping to her, scraping to her
Madam, says I, and made a bow
I'd quite forgot the weather
If ye'd permission nobbut give
I'd see ye home where'er you live.
With that she clicked me by the sleeve
And off we trudged together.

A bonny wild goose chase had we
In and out so, in and out so
A bonny wild goose chase had we
The London stones so galled me
At last she took me to a door
Where twenty lasses, aye, and more
Came out to have a better gloar
At Bumpkin, as they called me.

Walk in, kind sir, she said to me
Quite politely, quite politely
Walk in, kind sir, she said to me
Folks said, Poor lad, he's undone.
Walk in, said she. Not so, said I
For I have other fish to fry
So, having seen you home, goodbye!
I'ze Yorkshire, though in Lunnon.

My pockets soon I rummaged o'er
Cautious ever, cautious ever
My pockets soon I rummaged o'er
And found a diamond ring there
For I had this precaution took
In each to stitch a small fish hook
So when she groped for pocketbook
The barb it stripped her finger.

Three weeks I've been in London town
Living idle, living idle
Three weeks I've been in London town
It's time to pack to work, sir
The ring I've sold and got the brass
I haven't played the silly ass
'Twill serve to toast the London lass
When I get back to Yorkshire.

IF I WAS A BLACKBIRD

Tune: GG/1/7/356, Miss Lee; Text: GG/1/7/355, Henry Lee, both of Whitchurch, Hampshire, May 1906.

I'm only a poor girl and my fortune seems sad
Six months have I courted a young sailor lad
And truly I loved him by night and by day
And now in his transport he's sailed far away.

Chorus: *If I was a blackbird, could whistle and sing*
I'd follow the vessel my true-love sails in
And on the top rigging there I'd build my nest
And lay my head all night on his lily-white breast.

My love's tall and handsome in every degree
His parents despise him because he loves me
But let them despise him or say what they will
While I've breath in my body I'll love my man still.

He promised he'd meet me at Donnybrook fair
With a bunch of blue ribbon to tie up my hair
And if he would meet me I'd crown him with joy
And kiss those fond lips of my dear sailor boy.

If I was a scholar, could handle my pen
Just one private letter to him I would send
I'd write and I'd tell him of my sad grief and woe
And far o'er the water with him I would go.

IN A BRITISH MAN-O'-WAR (THE BRITISH MAN-OF-WAR)

GG/1/6/325, George Blake, St Denys, Southampton, Hampshire, June 1906.

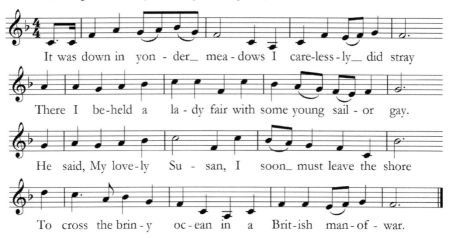

It was down in yonder meadows I carelessly did stray
There I beheld a lady fair with some young sailor gay.
He said, My lovely Susan, I soon must leave the shore
To cross the briny ocean in a British man-of-war.

Pretty Susan fell to weeping, Young sailor, she did say
How can you be so venturesome to throw yourself away
For it's when that I am twenty-one I shall receive my store
Jolly sailor, do not venture on a British man-of-war.

O Susan, lovely Susan, the truth to you I'll tell
The British flag insulted is, old England knows it well
I may be crowned with laurels, so like a jolly tar
I'll face the walls of China in a British man-of-war.

O sailor, do not venture to face the proud Chinese
For they will prove as treacherous as any Portuguese
And by some deadly dagger you may receive a scar
So it's turn your inclination from a British man-of-war.

O Susan, lovely Susan, the time will quickly pass
You come down to the ferry house to take a parting glass
For my shipmates they are waiting to row me from the shore
And it's for old England's glory in a British man-of-war.

The sailor took his handkerchief and cut it fair in two
Saying, Susan, take one half from me, I'll do the same by you
The bullets may surround me and cannons loudly roar
I'll fight for fame and Susan in a British man-of-war.

Then a few more words together when her love let go her hand
A jovial crew, they launched the boat and merrily went from land
The sailor waved his handkerchief when far away from shore
Pretty Susan blessed her sailor in a British man-of-war.

JOHN WHITE

HAM/5/56/10, Martha Russell, Upwey, Dorset, December 1907.

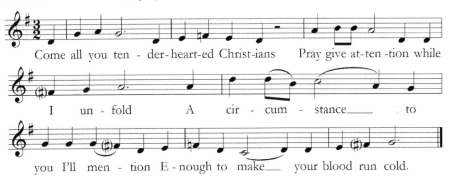

Come all you ten-der-heart-ed Christ-ians Pray give at-ten-tion while
I un-fold A cir-cum-stance to
you I'll men-tion E-nough to make your blood run cold.

Come all you tender-hearted Christians
Pray give attention while I unfold
A circumstance to you I'll mention
Enough to make your blood run cold.

John White was born of Irish parents
Brought up and reared in the town of Leeds
Where he enlisted there as a soldier
His mother's heart for him did sorely bleed.

For only striking a colour sergeant
He fell a victim, though not in war
And sentenced was to three hundred lashes
The bugle-horns did sound alarm.

When this clever young man all cut and
  mangled
Had fell quite lifeless to the ground
The cries and weeping of all beholders
Sad grief and anguish they did abound.

The mother weeping, the father distracted
To see their son all cut and scarred
Each one lamenting and still condoling
The afflicted parents of this bold hussar.

Come sign and send a long petition
To England's queen, the crowned head of
  wars
Pray never let a gallant soldier
Die like John White of the Seventh
  Hussars.

JOHNNY SANDS AND BETSY HAIGH (JOHNNY SANDS)

HAM/4/21/4, Mr Chard, Netherbury, Dorset, June 1906.

A man whose name was Johnny Sands
Had married Betsy Haigh.
And though she brought him gold and
lands
She proved an awful plague
She proved an awful plague.

For oh she was a scolding wife
Full of caprice and whim
He said that he was tired of life
And she was tired of him
And she was tired of him.

Says he, Then I will drown myself
The river runs below.
Says she, Pray do, you silly elf
I wished it long ago
I wished it long ago.

For fear that I should courage lack
And try to save my life
Pray tie my hands behind my back.
I will, replied his wife
I will, replied his wife.

So she tied them tight, as you may think
And when securely done
Now stand, says she, upon the brink
And I'll prepare to run
And I'll prepare to run.

All down the hill his loving bride
Now ran with all her force
To push him, he stepped aside
And she fell in of course
And she fell in of course.

Now splashing, dashing like a fish
Oh save me, Johnny Sands!
I can't, my dear, though much I wish
For you have tied my hands
For you have tied my hands.

JOLLY JOE, THE COLLIER'S SON

Tune: GG/1/7/351, Henry Lee, Whitchurch, Hampshire, June 1906.
Text: GG/1/7/351; stanza 2, lines 5–8 from HAM/2/10/21, Robert Barratt, Piddletown, Dorset,
September/October 1905.

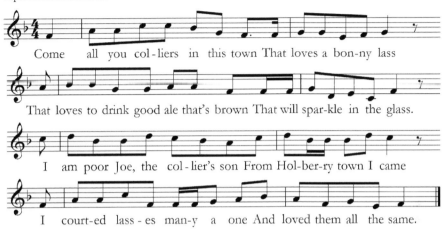

Come all you col-liers in this town That loves a bon-ny lass
That loves to drink good ale that's brown That will spar-kle in the glass.
I am poor Joe, the col-lier's son From Hol-ber-ry town I came
I court-ed lass-es man-y a one And loved them all the same.

Come all you colliers in this town
That loves a bonny lass
That loves to drink good ale that's brown
That will sparkle in the glass
I am poor Joe, the collier's son
From Holberry town I came
I courted lasses many a one
And loved them all the same.

I courted Nancy and young Kate
And buxom Nelly too
But Rachel's the girl I do admire
And that you soon shall know
My parents they all frowns on me
Saying I am much to blame
For keeping Rachel's company
'Twill bring me to grief and shame.

I took my walk from Holberry town
All round by Bilsom Hill
Who should I spy but my own true-love
With Jack of Amber's Mill
I hid myself all in the grove
A distance from where they were
He gave her kisses, one, two, and three
Not knowing that I was there.

I boldly stepped up to him
Saying, Thou rogue, what hast thou done?
I'm jolly Joe, the collier's son
Thou shalt either fight or run.
My fingers they began to itch
I scarce could hold them still
And presently I began to thump
Poor Jack of Amber's Mill.

Hold your hand, dear Joe, she said
No more of it I'll have
I'll be your servant, slave, and wife
Till we both go to the grave.
Then to the church poor Rachel went
Right sore against her will
So maidens, pity my downfall
And Jack's of Amber's Mill.

85

KING HENRY'S THREE SONS (IN GOOD KING ARTHUR'S DAYS)

GG/1/20/1239, Frank Harrington, Bartley, Hampshire, September 1908.

In old King Henry's reign
And a good old king was he
He had three sons in all and he turned them out of door
'Twas because they would not sing.
'Twas because they would not sing
'Twas because they would not sing.
He had three sons in all and he turned them out of door
'Twas because they would not sing.

Oh the first he was a miller
And the second he was a weaver
And the third he was a little tailor
So these three rogues went together
So these three rogues went together, etc.

Now the miller he stole corn
And the weaver he stole yarn
And the little tailor, oh he stole broadcloth
For to keep those three rogues warm
For to keep those three rogues warm, etc.

Now the miller got drowned in his dam
And the weaver got hung in his yarn
And the Devil ran away with the little tailor
With the broadcloth under his arm
With the broadcloth under his arm, etc.

THE LADY OF RICHES (THE PRESS GANG, I)

Tune and Text: HAM/4/23/2, Mrs Tuck, Beaminster, Dorset, June 1906. Stanza 8: HAM/5/36/13, Mrs Russell, Upwey, Dorset, December 1907. Stanzas 2, 5, 6, 7, 9, 10, 11 and 13 from various broadsides.

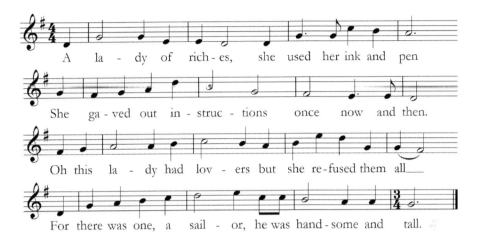

A lady of riches, she used her ink and pen
She gaved out instructions once now and then.
Oh this lady had lovers but she refused them all
For there was one, a sailor, he was handsome and tall.

At last her old father got word on the sly
That on a young sailor she had cast an eye
Never mind, said her father, I will them soon part
I'll seem to prove kind, though 'tis not in my heart.

Oh her father came unto her one day with a frown.
Is there no lord or squire around you to be found?
Is there no lord or squire to enjoy your sweet face
But to marry with a sailor your friends to disgrace?

Oh yes, dear honoured father, there's plenty whom I see
But not one in the world do I fancy but he
For he is my jewel and I am his joy
If I cannot have my sailor, my life I'll destroy.

O daughter, dearest daughter, since that is your lot
To marry a sailor, I'll forbid it not
But do so in private, say nothing to me
And when it is over we'll bravely agree.

This young lady's father was grieved to the heart
To think how to cause this young couple to part.
If it cost me ten hundred bright guineas, said he
I'll send for the press gang and force him to sea.

As they were a-walking towards the church door
The press gang did meet them, 'twas near to a score
Instead of being married he was pressed away
Instead of great joy there was a sorrowful day.

Then she plucked up her courage and changed her clothes
And in a man's apparel to the press gang she goes
And soon you shall hear how it fell to her lot
To be her love's messmate, though he knew it not.

Many a long night by her sailor she did lie
And little did he think that his true-love was so nigh
I once had a sweetheart in London, said he
But her cruel father has pressed me to sea.

She said, 'Tis well known I can act with my pen
An astrologer's part I can take now and then
Pray tell me your age and I'll cast out your lot
For to see if you will marry with your true-love or not.

He told her his age and the date of his birth.
She told to him his fortune, a great deal of worth
She told to him his fortune, she said, This is your lot
For I am your true-love, though you knew it not.

Oh the parson was sent for and sent for with speed
And then this young sailor he married her indeed
And now, my dear, I'm married, and married unto you
Here's a fig for your father and all he can do.

Now when this young couple returned to the land
Her father was dead, as we understand
And she was the heiress of her father's estate
And he was a lord of riches so great.

THE LAKE OF COLEPHIN (THE LAKES OF COOLFIN)

HAM/3/12/3, George Hatherill, Bath, Somerset, January 1906.

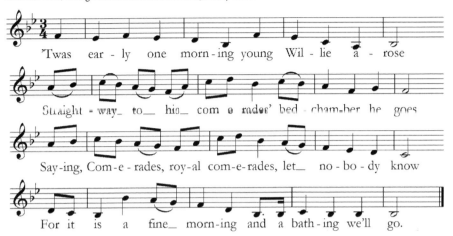

'Twas early one morning young Willie arose
Straightway to his comerade's bedchamber he goes
Saying, Comerades, royal comerades, let nobody know
For it is a fine morning and a-bathing we'll go.

They walked straight along till they came to a long lane
And the first that they met was a keeper of game
He warned them with sorrow for to turn back again
For there's deep and false water in the lake of Colephin.

Young Willie stripped off and he swam the lake round
He swum round the island, but not the right ground
Oh comrades, royal comrades, do not venture in
For there's deep and false water in the lake of Colephin.

The very next morning his sister arose
Straightway to her mother's bedchamber she goes
Saying, Mother, o mother, I've had a sad dream
Young Willie's a-floating in the watery stream.

The very next morning his mother came there
She had rings on every finger and tearing of her hair
Crying, Murder, oh murder, was there nobody nigh
To save the sweet life of my own darling boy?

The very next morning his uncle came there
He rode round the lake like a man in despair
Saying, Where was he drownded? or did he fall in?
There's deep and false waters in the lake of Colephin.

The very next morning his sweetheart arose
And straight to his mother in despair she goes
For every other morning he did her salute
With a bunch of red roses or fine garden fruit.

On the day of his funeral it was a grand sight
Twenty-four young men all dressed up in white
They carried him along and laid him in cold clay
Saying, Adieu to young William, and then marched away.

THE LASS OF LONDON CITY

Tune: GG/1/10/599, Alfred Porter, Basingstoke, Hampshire, October 1906.
Text: GG/1/10/599; augmented from a broadside by J. Pitts, London (British Library, 1875.d.5.(32.)); stanza 4
composed by Purslow.

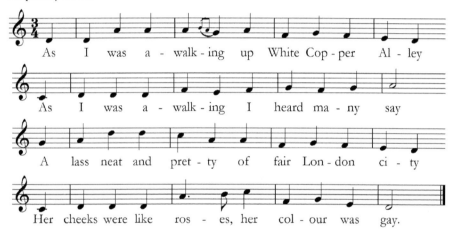

As I was a-walking up White Copper Alley
As I was a-walking I heard many say
A lass neat and pretty of fair London city
Her cheeks were like roses, her colour was gay.

I stepped up to her thinking to view her
Saying, Where are you going, my pretty maid?
Many kisses I vended and love I pretended
But all was in vain for she was a maid.

I must not, I will not, I shall not, I dare not
Submit to your passions for I am afraid
Should my friends then discover I have a new lover
Oh then they would call me a wanton young jade.

(I said, But my dear, there is no need to fear
We will go to some inn where we shall not be known.
'Twas then she relented, at last she consented
But first, gentle sir, some money pay down.)

Hearing these words made me more anxious than ever
To think I could purchase such a fair pretty maid
Five guineas she demanded, the money was granted
Supper being over, I put madam to bed.

But I being tired and weary of drinking
But I being tired and weary of play
Oh I fell a-nodding and she fell a-robbing
And quitted my bedroom before it was day.

I turned round to kiss her and suddenly I missed her
I looked for my wallet* right under my head
But she'd robbed and she'd plundered, I roared out like thunder
But all was in vain for madam was fled.

It's not my gold watch nor my money I value
It's not my gold watch nor my money I crave
For I'm afraid some young doctor will be my conductor
I wish I had never seen that pretty fair maid.

*Alfred Porter's text has ticker, a corruption of kickster on the ballad sheet, a slang name for a
  wallet

THE *LONDON* MAN-O'-WAR

Tune and Text: GG/1/3/85, Richard Hall, Itchen Abbas, Hampshire, 1905. Stanza 6 and a few lines from
GG/1/20/1270, James Blooming, Upper Farringdon, Hampshire, October 1908.

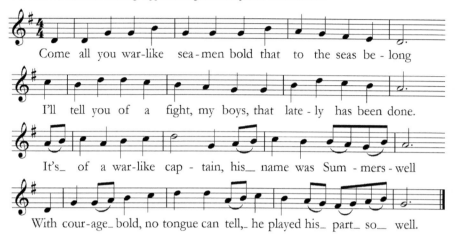

Come all you warlike seamen bold that to the seas belong
I'll tell you of a fight, my boys, that lately has been done.
It's of a warlike captain, his name was Summerswell
With courage bold, no tongue can tell, he played his part so well.

On the fifteenth of September near Spithead we did lay
There came on board an order, we could no longer stay
All off the coast of Ireland, our order did run so
'Twas there to fight and not refuse to face our daring foe.

We had not long been on the sea before a sail we spied
A small ship from the westward came bearing down that side
They hailed us in French, my boys, to know from whence we came
Our answer was from Liverpool and the London was our name.

Are you a man-o'-war, sir, or pray what may you be?
Oh yes, replied our captain, and that you soon may see.
Then haul down your English colours and make your ship bring to
If we be stout, you must be stouter, or else we will sink you.

That's very well, that's very well, our captain he did say
Cheer up, cheer up, my merry men, we'll show them British play
Whichever shall be master the truth shall soon be tried
Let every man stand true to his gun, we'll give them a broadside.

The first broadside we gave to them we made them for to wonder
To see their lofty main tops'ls come rattling down like thunder
We drove them from their quarters where they could no longer stay
Our guns did roar, we played so sure, we showed them British play.

So now we've gained the victory, the heavens did prove kind
We'll go to Plymouth harbour and drink a glass of wine
Here's a health unto our captain and all such warlike souls
To him we'll drink and never flinch out of a flowing bowl.

LONG LOOKED FOR, COME AT LAST

Tune: GG/1/10/618, William Winter, Andover, Hampshire, July 1906.
Text: GG/1/10/618; augmented from a version noted by Alfred Williams from Jane Wall, Driffield,
Gloucestershire (Alfred Williams MS Collection, Gl 79).

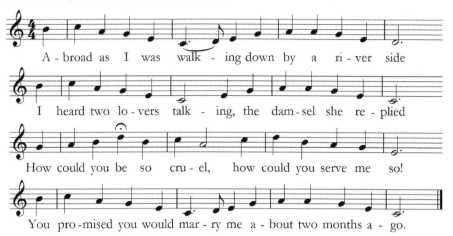

Abroad as I was walking down by a river side
I heard two lovers talking, the damsel she replied
How could you be so cruel, how could you serve me so!
You promised you would marry me about two months ago.

My dear, I was prevented and could not come till now
So rest yourself contented, I never will break my vow
If I'd all the gold and silver that lies beyond the sea
I'd take more joy and pleasure in your sweet company.

What maiden can believe you? you've said so much before
The last time that I saw you, you said you'd come no more
You went and courted Nancy, the girl with a rolling eye
It's she alone you fancy, you cannot this deny.

I hear to what you say, my love, I own and swear 'tis true
I went and courted Nancy, but now I'm come to you
Why should it breed a faction betwixt my love and I?
It's you, my dear, I fancy, with you I'll live and die.

These words they revived her and struck her to the heart
And we will have the wedding before that we do part
The weather being pleasant, to church this couple passed
And now they are got married, long looked for, come at last.

LORD RENDAL (LORD RANDAL)

HAM/2/6/21, Miss Brown, Lydlinch, Dorset, 1905.

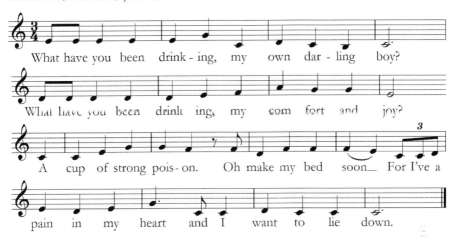

What have you been drinking, my own darling boy?
What have you been drinking, my comfort and joy?
A cup of strong poison. Oh make my bed soon
For I've a pain in my heart and I want to lie down.

What will you leave your mother, my own darling boy?
What will you leave your mother, my comfort and joy?
I'll leave her my love, oh make my bed soon
For I've a pain in my heart and I want to lie down.

What will you leave your sister, my own darling boy?
What will you leave your sister, my comfort and joy?
I'll leave her my money, oh make my bed soon
For I've a pain in my heart and I want to lie down.

What will you leave your brother, my own darling boy?
What will you leave your brother, my comfort and joy?
I'll leave him my gold watch, oh make my bed soon
For I've a pain in my heart and I want to lie down.

What will you leave your sweetheart, my own darling boy?
What will you leave your sweetheart, my comfort and joy?
I'll leave her the gallows, oh make my bed soon
For I've a pain in my heart and I want to lie down.

Where will you be buried, my own dear darling boy?
Where will you be buried, my comfort and joy?
Away in green meadows where grass grows sweet
There lay me down to have a long sleep.

LOW DOWN IN THE BROOM

Tune: GG/1/8/460, George Smith, Fareham, Hampshire, July 1906.
Text: stanzas 1 and 7 from GG/1/8/460; stanzas 3 and 4 from GG/1/15/948, James Channon, Ellisfield, by
Basingstoke, Hampshire, September 1907; stanzas 2, 5, and 6 from a broadside without imprint (British Library,
1876.e.20.(34a.)).

'Twas on last Easter Monday, the day appointed was
For me to go down in the broom to meet my bonny lass
How sweet and pleasant was the day I kept her company
She was low, low down in the broom a-waiting there for me.

I turned myself all round about to see what I could see
And there I saw my own true-love come wandering down to me
I kindly took her by the hand and gave her kisses three
And it's low, low down in the broom my true-love went with me.

I took her by the lily-white hand and said, My own sweetheart
Since you and I together have met I hope we never shall part
I hope we never shall part, my love, until the day we die
We'll go again down in the broom and married we will be.

She said, Young man, leave go my hands, for I'm sure it will never be so
For little does my mother think, nor yet my father know
It often does run in their minds what will become of me
They little know I'm in the broom a-talking along with thee.

I took her round the middle so small and gently laid her down
And these were the words she said to me as she lay in the broom
Do what you will, young man, she said, 'tis all the same to me
For little does my mother think that I'm in the broom with thee.

My father is a miser and will not give me gold
My mother is a scolding dame and does the house control
But I will love my bonny lad until the day I die
And it's low, low down in the broom he'll be waiting there for me.

I gave my love a parting kiss and homewards I returned
I told her to remember our meeting in the broom
For what was done and what was said, 'twas all as one to me
But I'll call again down in the broom and so merrily we will be.

MADAM, I WILL GIVE TO THEE (THE KEYS OF HEAVEN)

Tune and Text: HAM/2/2/24, Mrs Gulliver, Combe Florey, Somerset, 1905. Final stanza: HAM /4/23/24, D563, Mrs Farnham, South Perrot, Dorset.

O madam, I will give to thee a new silken gown
With five and thirty flounces a-bobbing to the ground
If you will be my bride,* my joy, and my dear
If you'll go a-walking with me anywhere.

No, indeed, I won't accept of your new silken gown
With five and thirty flounces a-bobbing to the ground
I won't be your bride, nor your joy, nor your dear
I won't go a-walking with you anywhere.

O man Jan, what can the matter be?
You see, I love this lady but she won't love me
She won't be my bride, my joy, or my dear
She won't go a-walking with me anywhere.

Oh you court her, master, you court her, never fear
For she'll be your bride and your joy and your dear
Yes, she'll be your bride and your joy and your dear
She'll go a-walking with you anywhere.

The rest of the song follows the above pattern:

... a fine knit cap
With ribbon on the border and netting on the top.

... a little greyhound
Of every hair upon his back 'tis worth a thousand pound.

… a bed of down so soft
And you shall lie under and I shall lie aloft.

… a little set of bells
For to call up your servants when you're not very well.

… a cushion full of pins
For to pin up the baby's white musselins.

… the keys of my heart
To lock it up together and never more depart. **

This time the lady accepts:

Yes, indeed, I will accept the keys of thy heart
I'll lock it up forever and nevermore depart
For if you'll be my love, my joy, and my dear
Oh I'll go a-walking with you anywhere.

O man Jan, here's forty pound for thee
I shouldn't 'a' had this lady dear if it hadn't been for thee
And now she's my love, my joy, and my dear
And she'll go a-walking with me anywhere.

* or love
** perhaps To lock us up together and never more to part

MADAM, MADAM, I'M COME A-COURTING (RIPEST APPLES)

Tune and stanza 2: HAM/5/36/4, Mrs Russell, Upwey, Dorset, December 1907. Stanzas 1, 5 and 7: GG/1/9/491, Charles Chivers, Basingstoke, Hampshire, August 1908. Stanzas 3, 4 and 6: GG/1/2/62, William Smith, Twyford, Hampshire, June 1905.

Yonder sits a fair pretty virgin
Who she is I do not know
I'll go and court her for her beauty
Let her answer me yes or no.

Chorus: *Fal dal the dee, rite fal the dee*
Fal dal the diddle al the di gee o.

Madam, I am come a-courting
If your favour I can gain.
Sit you down, you're kindly welcome.
Use me well, I'll come again.

Madam, I've got gold and silver
Madam, I've got houses and land
Madam, I've got a world of treasure
All it is at your command.

I don't want your gold and silver
I don't want your houses and land
I don't want the world of treasure
All I want is a handsome man.

Madam, don't think so much about beauty
Beauty's a thing that will soon decay
For the finest of flowers that shines in the
    summer
Dies away on a cold winter's day.

Long-gathered apples soon get rotten
Hottest love soon gets cold
Young men's words are soon forgotten
Pray, pretty maid, don't be too bold.

First come cowslips, then come daisies
And after night, then come day
After false love, then comes a true-love
See how it pass a little time away.

THE MAN OF DOVER (BIRMINGHAM BOYS)

Tune: HAM/3/17/4, John Pomery (of Broad Oak) in Bridport Union, Dorset, May 1906.
Text: HAM/3/17/4; second half of stanza 8 and stanzas 10, 11, and 14 from HAM/2/1/15, Mrs Gulliver, Combe
Florey, Somerset, April/May 1905; stanza 15 from HAM/5/33/49, Marina Russell, Upwey, Dorset,
January/February 1907; stanzas 9, 12, and 13 from Harry Cox, Norfolk.

There was a man in Dover, he had a loving wife
And she did love bad company so dear as she loved her life.

Whilst this poor man goes on the sea his living for to get
While he gets one penny she spends three, that's all for the want of wit.

When the poor man came home from sea, 'twas late all in the night
Enquiring for his own dear wife, his joy and heart's delight.

He said unto the maid, Where is your mistress gone?
She's gone unto some neighbour's house, shall I go fetch her home?

He sat there awhile till he began to think
Oh no, my dear, I'll go myself for I do intend to drink.

As he was going up Dover street, there he heard a terrible noise
And there he did spy his own dear wife along with the Dover boys.

He heard her say, Come in, my dear, and sit you down by me
For we will spend our money free what our husbands get on the sea.

Come fill us up another quart, let us see what we have to pay
There's not a man among you all but has kissed me once today.

Then this poor man he went back home, his heart was nearly broke
And when he had sent out the maid then he prepared a rope.

And when his wife came to the house she run to him with a kiss
Saying, You're welcome home, dear husband, so long a time you have been missed.

Go and bolt the doors all round, said he, and see they're all quite fast
Not a kick nor bruise shall never take place so long as the rope shall last.

He beat her once, he beat her twice, till she was wonderful sore
Till she cries out, O husband dear, I'll never do so no more.

And if you do, I'll make you rue and curse the hour you were born
For cuckolding of your husband dear, I'll make you wear the horns.

So come all you women of Dover, a warning take by me
Don't never cuckold your husband while he is gone to sea.

For I have cuckolded mine for seven long years or more
And now I have to suffer for my backside is sore.

MATHEW THE MILLER

HAM/4/21/12, John Hallett, Mosterton, Dorset, June 1906.

I clapped my hand up-on her toe. What's this, my love, what's this, my
dear? 'Tis my toe-a-tap, I go leer Toe-a tap, tit-a-tap-
-in Where Mat-hew the mill-er the malt grinds in.

*sing this bar as many times as required – once in the first stanza, twice in the second and so on

I clapped my hand upon her toe
What's this, my love, what's this, my dear?
'Tis my toe-a-tap, I go leer
Toe-a-tap, tit-a-tap-in
Where Mathew the miller the malt grinds in.

I clapped my hand upon her knee
What's this, my love, what's this, my dear?
'Tis my knee-a-nap, I go leer
Knee-a-nap, toe-a-tap, tit-a-tap-in
Where Mathew the miller the malt grinds in.

I clapped my hand upon her thigh.
What's this, my love, what's this, my dear?
'Tis my thigh-a-nap, I go leer
Thigh-a-nap, knee-a-nap, toe-a-tap, tit-a-tap-in
Where Mathew the miller the malt grinds in.

The song then accumulates after the above pattern as follows:

rump	swagger-arse
belly	plimp-sack
breast	bumpers
neck	gudgel-pipe
chin	chin-a-chop
mouth	grinders
nose	snorters
eyes	lookers
head	raggy locks

THE MERRY CUCKOLD (OUR GOODMAN)

HAM/3/19/16, Simeon Symonds, Whitchurch, Dorset, May 1906.

As I went into my stable, oh there did I see
Gentlemen's horses standing there by one, by two, by three.
I called unto my loving wife and unto her did say
How came these gentlemen's horses here without the leave of me?
You old cuckold, you blind cuckold
And cannot you very well see
'Tis three lofty milking cows
My mother has sent to me.

Chorus: *Hey bobs! There's fun*
Milking cows with saddles on!
Like was never seen
And ev'ry time that I go out, a cuckold I come in.

Subsequent verses follow the same pattern:

As I went into my passage, oh…
Gentlemen's hats a-hanging there…
'Tis three lofty milking pails…
 Milking pails with brims on.

As I went into my entery, oh…
Gentlemen's coats a-hanging there…
'Tis three lofty milking cloaks…
 Milking cloaks with sleeves on.

As I went into my kitchen, oh…
Gentlemen's boots a-lying there…
'Tis three lofty pudding bags…
 Pudding bags with spurs on!

As I went into my parlour, oh…
Gentlemen's watches hanging there…
'Tis three lofty cheese vits*…
 Cheese vits with chains on.

As I went into my chamber, oh there did I see
Gentlemen lying there by one, by two, by three
I called unto my loving wife and unto her did say
How came these gentlemen lying here without the leave of me?
You old cuckold, you blind cuckold
And cannot you very well see
'Tis three lofty milking maids
My mother has sent to me.

Chorus: *Hey bobs! There's fun*
Milking maids with beards on!
Like was never seen
And every time that I go out, a cuckold I come in.

*cheese vats or presses

105

MOLLY AND WILLIAM (FALSE-HEARTED WILLIAM)

Tune: HAM/5/32/16, Marina Russell, Upwey, Dorset, January 1907.
Text: HAM/5/32/16; stanza 2 and second half of stanza 4 from HAM/3/17/6, John Pomery (of Broad Oak),
Bridport Union, Dorset, May 1906.

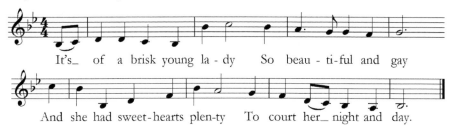

It's_ of a brisk young la - dy So beau - ti-ful and gay
And she had sweet-hearts plen-ty To court her_ night and day.

It's of a brisk young lady
So beautiful and gay
And she had sweethearts plenty
To court her night and day.

The first that came a-courting
It was a farmer's son
Love me, love me, dear Molly
Or distracted I shall run.

She had not long been courted
Before with child she proved
She lived so discontented
She told it to her love.

O William, dearest William
I am with child by thee
I'll have you seek for licence
And quickly marry me.

O Molly, dearest Molly
Since you've a-run such risk
I can't no more admire
Your sweet and charming face.

Then up and down she wandered
Trying to hide her shame
Till at length herself she drownded
For the sake of sweet William.

Come all you constant lovers
That have a mind to love
Be constant and true-hearted
And sure that you love for love.

THE MURDERED SERVANT-MAN (BRUTON TOWN)

Tune: GG/1/16/984, Mrs Randall, Preston Candover, Hampshire, October 1907. Text: GG/1/4/208, George Digweed, Micheldever, Hampshire, March 1907, with stanza 4 and slight amendments to stanzas 1, 2, 3 and 5 from: GG/1/12/757, Daniel Wigg, Preston Candover, Hampshire, July 1907.

A famous farmer as you shall hear
He had two sons and one daughter dear
Her servant-man she much admired
None in the world she loved so dear.
One of these brothers said to the other
See how our sister's going to wed
Let all such courtship soon be ended
We'll hoist him to some silent grave.

They asked of him to go a-hunting
He went without any fear or strife
Then these two jewels proved so cruel
They took away this young man's life.
It was near the creek where there is no
  water
Nothing but bushes and briars grew
All for to hide their cruel slaughter
Into the bushes his body threw.

When they returned from the field of
  hunting
She began to enquire for her servant-man
Come, brothers, tell me because you
  whisper
Come, brothers, tell me if you can.
Why, sister, we are so much amazed
To see you look so much at we
We left him in the field of hunting
No more of him then could we see.

As she lay musing on her pillow
She dreamed she saw her true-love stand
By her bedside he stood lamenting
All covered with some bloody wounds.
Pray, Nancy dear, don't you weep for me
Pray, Nancy dear, don't weep nor pine
In that creek where there is no water
Go there, you may my body find.

Then she rose early the very next morning
With many a sigh and bitter groan
In that creek where her true-love told her
There she found his body thrown.
The blood all on his lips was drying
His tears were salter than any brine
Then she kissed him, loudly crying
Here lies a bosom friend of mine.

Three nights and days she stayed
  lamenting
Till her poor heart was filled with woe
Until sharp hunger came creeping on her
Then homeward she was forced to go.
Sister, we are so much amazed
To see you look so pale and wan.
Brothers, I know you know the reason
And for the same you shall be hung.

To second part of tune:

Then these two brothers both were taken
And bound all down in some prison strong
They both were tried, found out as guilty
And for the same they both were hung.

My Good Old Man (Good Old Man)

GG/1/2/23, E. Quintrell, Helston, Cornwall who learned it from Miss Fanny Stevens of Talstaddy, St. Columb, Cornwall, who died in 1885, aged 93.

She: What will you have for supper, my good old man?
What will you have for supper? She called him her lamb.
What will you have for supper, my loving husband?
  You're the sweetest old man that's alive, alive, alive
  You're the sweetest old man that's alive.
He: Three score eggs, my dear, and fol de dol de dee
  Fol dol diddle dol de dee
Three score eggs, my dear, and fol de dol de dee
  Fol dol diddle dol de dee.

She: That will make you sick, etc.
He: Then I shall be dead, my dear, etc.

She: And where will you be buried, etc.
He: In the chimney corner, my dear, etc.

She: What will you be buried there for, etc.
He: To see you play and flirt, my dear, etc.

She: I never did but once, my good old man
I never did but twice. She called him her lamb.
I never did but three times, my loving husband
    You're the sweetest old man that's alive, etc.
He: Then who was it with, my dear, etc.

She: Once with the parson, my good old man.
Twice with the clerk. She called him her lamb.
Three times with the sexton, my loving husband
    You're the sweetest old man that's alive, alive, alive
    You're the sweetest old man that's alive.

MY HUSBAND'S GOT NO COURAGE IN HIM (O DEAR O)

Tune: HAM/4/28/37, Jesse Steer, Stratton, Dorset, November 1906.
Text: HAM/4/28/37; stanza 5 and some slight amendments from a broadside.

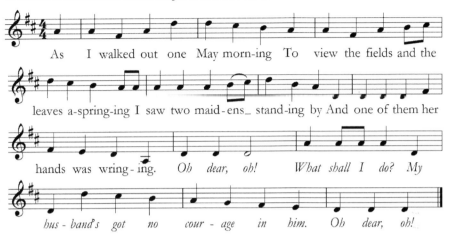

As I walked out one May morning
To view the fields and the leaves a-
   springing
I saw two maidens standing by
And one of them her hands was wringing.

Chorus: *Oh dear, oh!*
What shall I do?
My husband's got no courage in him.
Oh dear, oh!

All sorts of victuals* I did provide
All sorts of meats that's fitting for him
With oyster pie and rhubarb too
But nothing will put courage in him.

My husband can dance and caper and sing
Or do anything that is fitting for him
But he cannot do the thing that I want
Because he has no courage in him.

My husband's admired wherever he goes
And everyone looks well upon him
With his handsome features and well-
   shaped leg
But still he has no courage in him.

Seven long years I've made his bed
And every night I've laid aside him
But this morning I rose with my
   maidenhead
For still he has no courage in him.

I wish my husband he was dead
And in the grave I'd quickly lay him
Then I'd try some other one
That's got some little courage in him.

*pronounced 'vittals', which is what Purslow
printed*

My Jolly Roving Tar (The Jolly Roving Tar)

Tune and the second half of stanza 1, and all of stanza 3: HAM/4/29/26, Mrs J. Seale in Dorchester Union, Dorset, December 1906.

Text: GG/1/11/657, George Hiscock, Minstead, Lyndhurst, Hampshire, November 1906.

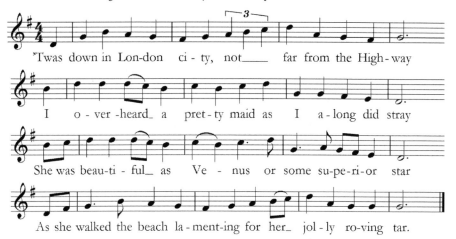

'Twas down in London city, not far from the Highway
I overheard a pretty maid as I along did stray
She was beautiful as Venus or some superior star
As she walked the beach lamenting for her jolly roving tar.

Oh William, gallant William, how could you sail away?
When I arrive at twenty-one I am a lady gay
I'll man one of my father's ships and brave the chains of war
I'll cross the briny ocean for my jolly roving tar.

If I could see my William dressed in his sailor's clothes
His cheeks as red as roses and his eyes as black as sloes
Oh his hair hung down in ringlets, now he's gone from me afar
But my heart lies in the bosom of my jolly roving tar.

It's many a pleasant evening my love and I have passed
With many a jolly sailor and many a bonny lass
While the harps were sweetly playing, likewise the wild guitar
I went hand in hand together with my jolly roving tar.

Come, come, my jolly sailor lads and push this boat from shore
That I may view my father's ships and find they are secure
Provisions we have plenty and lots of grog in store
I'll give chase, my jolly sailors, for my jolly roving tar.

She stepped into the long boat and boldly left the land
And as the sailors rowed her she waved her lily hand
Farewell, you girls of London town, I fear no wound nor scar
And away went pretty Susan for her jolly roving tar.

NANCY (BEAUTIFUL NANCY, II)

Tune and Text: GG/1/18/1123, William Garrett, Petersfield Workhouse, Hampshire, August 1908, with stanzas 4 and 5 and other augmentations from: GG/1/5/273, Moses Blake, Emery Down, Lyndhurst, Hampshire, May 1906.

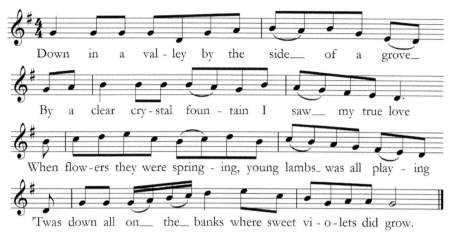

Down in a val-ley by the side of a grove
By a clear cry-stal foun-tain I saw my true love
When flow-ers they were spring-ing, young lambs was all play-ing
'Twas down all on the banks where sweet vi-o-lets did grow.

['Twas] down in a valley by the side of a grove
By a clear crystal fountain I saw my true-love
When flowers they were springing, young lambs was all playing
'Twas down all on the banks where sweet violets did grow.

The first time I saw my love she did my heart surprise
By the blooming of her cheeks and the sparkling of her eyes
Young Cupid so cruelly directed a dart
And the loss of young Nancy hath wounded my heart.

Bring me pen, ink, and paper that I may go and write
To my own dearest Nancy, my joy and heart's delight
Young Nancy is so charming, most beautiful and fair
There's no one in this country can with my love compare.

The birds on the branches are blessed with their mates
And the dove she is mourning for my unhappy fate
And the lark she is mounting in the high, lofty air
To bring me glad tidings of Nancy, my dear.

So now in these torments I'm forced to remain
Like a thief that is fettered and bound in some chains
No peace night or day can my heart ever find
For the loss of young Nancy hath troubled my mind.

Fare you well, my dearest Nancy, since parted we must be
I'm off to yon green mountain where no one shall me see
Where rocks they shall hide me and bring me to my grave
Fare you well, dearest Nancy, since you I cannot have.

THE 'NEW' DESERTER (THE DESERTER)

Tune: GG/1/9/509, James Brown, Basingstoke, Hampshire, August 1906.
Text: GG/1/9/509; slightly augmented from a broadside by H. Such.

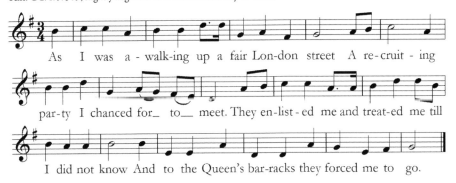

As I was a-walking up a fair London street
A recruiting party I chanced for to meet
They enlisted me and treated me till I did not know
And to the Queen's barracks they forced me to go.

The first time I deserted I thought myself free
But my cruel comrade informed against me
I was quickly followed after and brought back with speed
I was handcuffed, I was guarded, heavy irons on me.

Court martial, court martial they held upon me
And the sentence passed on me was three hundred and three
May the Lord have mercy on them for their sad cruelty
For you see the Queen's duty now lies heavy on me.

The next time I deserted I thought myself free
Till my cruel sweetheart informed against me
I was quickly followed after and brought back with speed
I was handcuffed, I was guarded, heavy irons on me.

Court martial, court martial was very soon got
And the sentence passed on me that I had to be shot
May the Lord have mercy on them for their sad cruelty
For you see the Queen's duty now lies heavy on me.

Now it's down comes Prince Albert in his carriage and six
Come, bring me out that young man whose coffin is fixed
Release him from his irons and let him go free
For he'll make a good soldier for his Queen and country.

Night Visit Song (Night Visiting Song)

GG/1/16/1014, William Stockley, Locksheath, Titchfield, Hampshire, September 1907.

The time is come, I must be go - ing The burn-ing temp - est I__
have to cross. All ov - er the moun - tains I've
rode_ with plea - sure This ve - ry night__ I'll be with my lass.

The time is come, I must be going
The burning tempest I have to cross.
All over the mountains I've rode with pleasure
This very night I'll be with my lass.

I came unto my true-love's window
I knelt down gently upon a stone
'Twas through a pane that I whispered slowly
Saying, My dear girl, are you alone?

She rose her head from her soft down pillow
Snowy was her milk-white breast
Crying, Who is there outside my window,
That have deprived me of my night's rest?

It's your true-love, do not discover
I pray, love, rise and let me in
I am fatigued after my long journey
Besides I'm wet unto the skin.

My love she rose with greatest pleasure
Opening the door for to let me in
We kissed, shook hands, embraced each other
Till that long night were at an end.

When that long night were gone and over
The cocks they did begin to crow
We kissed, shook hands, in sorrow parted
I took my leave and away did go.

My love has skin as the snow in winter
Her cheeks is red as the rose in June
Her black sparkling eye like a blazing star
In a winter's night and it freezes too.

THE NOBLEMAN AND THE THRESHER (THE NOBLEMAN AND THE THRESHERMAN)

Tune and the bulk of stanzas 1, 2 and 4: GG/1/20/1230, William Cole, East Stratton, Hampshire, September 1908, with stanzas 3 and 6 from: GG/1/10/629, William Stratton, Easton, Winchester, November 1906. Stanza 5 is a mixture of Stratton and: GG/1/7/411, Henry Stansbridge, Lyndhurst, Hampshire, June 1906.

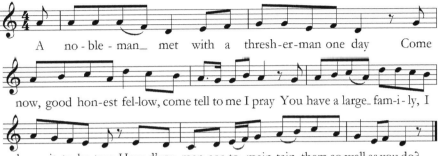

A noble-man_ met with a thresh-er-man one day   Come
now, good hon-est fel-low, come tell to me I pray   You have a large_ fam-i-ly, I
know it to be true   How d'you man-age to_ main-tain_them so well as you do?

A nobleman met with a thresher-man one day
Come now, good honest fellow, come tell to me I pray
You have a large family, I know it to be true
How d'you manage to maintain them so well as you do?

Why, sometimes I do reap and sometimes I do mow
Sometimes to hedging and a-ditching I do go
There's nothing comes amiss with me from the harrow to the plough
That's how I gets my living by the sweat of my brow.

My wife she is willing to join in the yoke
We live like two turtle doves and never do provoke
Although the times are hard and we are very poor
Yet we always keep the wolves and the ravens from the door.

When I go home of a night as tired as can be
I takes the youngest child and dandles it on my knee
The others gathers round with their pretty prattling toys
And that is all the comfort that a poor man enjoys.

Well done, my honest fellow, you speak well of your wife
Now I will make you happy all the days of your life
Here's fifty acres of good land I'll give it unto thee
For to maintain thy wife and thy sweet family.

So God bless thee, rich man, that considers a poor man
I hope that in heaven you'll get the upper hand
And those that's left behind, we're in hopes for to mend
That we might follow after as quick as we can.

OH DEAR, HOW I LONG TO GET MARRIED!

Tune: GG/1/6/303, George Blake, St Denys, Southampton, Hampshire, May 1906.
Text: GG/1/6/303; stanza 4 from Alfred Williams MS Collection, Mi 596 (source unknown).

I'm a damsel so blooming and gay
Who along with the females must mingle
It's a shocking bad thing, lackaday
When a maid is compelled to live single.
My age it's twenty and three
And of wedlock I fear I miscarry
Oh pray get a husband for me
For oh dear, how I long to get married.

Chorus: *I'm tired of living alone*
I'm tired of living alone.

I would make a most excellent wife
I would clean well the plates and the dishes
My husband I'd help into bed
Wash his shirt well and mend up his
    breeches
His breakfast up to his bedside
Every morning I speedily would carry.
I'd help for to dress him besides
For oh dear, how I long to get married.

I would marry a tinker or sweep
A dustman, cobbler, or tailor
A coal-heaver, butcher, or baker
A farmer, soldier, or sailor.
If he'd never a shirt to his back
Or a nose to his face, I'd him carry
To church any day in a crack
For oh dear, how I long to get married.

Whenever I'm left to myself
Just like an old witch I begin grumbling
I never can take any rest
From mumbling and tumbling and
    fumbling.
I will hang myself up to a tree
Before that much longer I've tarried
No pleasure at all can I see
For oh dear, how I long to get married.

OLD DADDY FOX (THE FOX)

Tune: GG/1/12/767, Sarah Goodyear, Axford, Hampshire, July 1907.
Text: GG/1/10/614, Stephen Phillimore, Andover, Hampshire, August 1906; with amendments from GG/1/12/767.

Old daddy fox walked out one moonshiny night
And he reared himself right bolt upright
Damme, says old Reynolds, I must have something nice
Against my laying down, o
Down, o, down, o
Damme, says old Reynolds, I must have something nice
Against my laying down, o.

He went on to the very next stile
And there he stood and considered for a while.
Damme, says old Reynolds, there's another half a mile
Before I get into the town, o
Town, o, town, o
Damme, says old Reynolds, there's another half a mile
Before I get into the town, o.

He travelled along till he came to the yard
The ducks and the geese they were all afeared
Says he, The fattest of all shall grease my grey beard
Before that I leaves this yard, o
Yard, o, yard, o, etc.

He catched the old grey goose by the neck
And he gave him a swing up over his back
The rest of them all went quickle, quack, quack
And his legs hung dangling down, o
Down, o, down, o, etc.

Old mother Wibble-Wobble jumped out of bed
Out of the window she popped her bushel head
Saying, Husband, o husband, the grey goose is dead
And the fox has gone over the downs, o
Downs, o, downs, o, etc.

The old man jumped up with his nightcap
Swore he would catch him in his trap
But the fox he's more wit and gave them the slip
And off he's gone over the downs, o
Downs, o, downs, o, etc.

Now the old man he went to the foot of the hill
And there he blew his horn both loud and shrill
Ah! says the fox, thy pretty music still
Shall carry me over the downs, o
Downs, o, downs, o, etc.

Then away he run till he came to his den
Where he had young ones, eight, nine, or ten
The youngest of them all says, Daddy, go again
For you brings us good meat from the town, o
Town, o, town, o, etc.

Oh no, oh no, that never can be
For the old bitch of hell she has twigged me
She swore she'd kill her husband if he didn't me
So I go no more to the town, o
Town, o, town, o, etc.

OLD MOTHER CRAWLEY

GG/1/7/401, George Lovett, Winchester, Hampshire, August 1906.

Oh come all you young seamen, I'd have you beware
Of old Mother Crawley I'd have you take care.
Of old Mother Rogers, so called by name
She goes a-bumboating, that noted fine game.

Chorus: *And sing tooral liday, rite tooral lay*
Rite tooral laddy, rite tooral liday.

Our ship has arrived safe brought up in the Sound
The tailors and the bumboats they all flock around
Alongside comes Mother Crawley with her bumboat of store
You're welcome, my children, to Plymouth once more.

She hands up the soft tack and butter also
And what else is wanted straightforward she'll go
There's soft tack, there's butter, there's sugar, there's tea
I know you young lads have been looking for me.

Soft tack is two shillings and butter is four
Two pounds of sausages five shillings more
Six eggs, fourteen pence, come, boys, be quick, for I'm thronged
Which makes twelve and twopence, so, Jack, jog along.

Early next morning on the quarterdeck she appears
Pity, kind gentle folks, both far and near
Your men owes me money, you see by this paper
They'll pay the girls first, they all swear by their maker.

And as for you, boatswain, I'm pretty well sure
You'll settle with me first and pay off your score
For it's this I will promise and that I will do
They are far better slops than you'll get from the Jew.

Our ship she's got orders for Botany Bay
The girls and the bumboats must all lose their pay
Our anchor's apeak, our ship she's wore round
Farewell, Mother Crawley, likewise Plymouth Sound.

OLD WOMAN'S SONG

GG/1/20/1310, Henry Purkiss[?], Cadnam, Hampshire, October 1908.

I am an old woman, you know
Four score years and one
Yet for that, you know
I can mark so straight as a gun.

Chorus: *Then lawk-a-messie what fun*
I pray to my soul
I'd never grow old
If kissing had never been done.

I am an old woman, you know
Four score years and two
Yet for that, you know
I can stoop to buckle my shoe.

Subsequent verses follow the same pattern:

Four score years and three
I can garter above my knee.

Four score years and four
I can cock my leg higher or lower.

Four score years and five
I can keep the game alive.

Four score years and six
I can stoop to pick up sticks.

Four score years and seven
I do pray to go to heaven.

Four score years and eight
I can bend my leg crooked or straight.

Four score years and nine
I can toss a glass of wine.

Four score years and ten
I do love to kiss the men.

POOR OLD HORSE

Tune: GG/1/19/1215, Richard Haynes, East Stratton, Hampshire, September 1908.
Text: GG/1/19/1215; stanza 3 and minor amendments from a broadside by Fortey (British Library, 11621.h.11, vol. 2, no. 4).

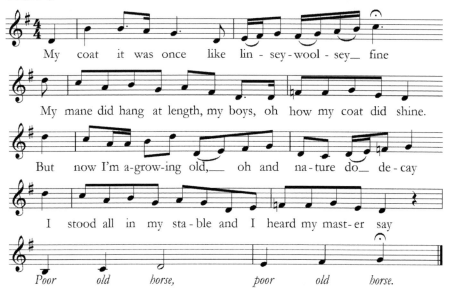

My coat it was once like linsey-woolsey fine
My mane did hang at length, my boys, oh how my coat did shine.
But now I'm a-growing old, oh and nature do decay
I stood all in my stable and I heard my master say
Poor old horse, poor old horse.

You eats all my hay and you spoils all my straw
Indeed you are not able my cart all for to draw
You are old and you are cold, you're lazy, dull and slow
So we'll whip him, cut him, skin him, to the hounds we'll let him go
Poor old horse, poor old horse.

My lodging was once all in a stable warm
To keep my tender limbs from cold and from harm
But now in open fields I'm forced for to go
To bear the cold winter's hail, rain and snow
Poor old horse, poor old horse.

Oh my food it was once the best of corn and hay
Besides the finest grass that grew in field or meadow gay
But now there's no such comforts as I can find at all
For I'm obliged to nip the short grass that grows against the wall
Poor old horse, poor old horse.

Oh my shoulders once were fat, fine, smooth, and round
But now I am turned out, my boys, corrupted and unsound
Here is my hollow hoof that once was smooth and hard
All by some roguish blacksmith is now most sadly shod
  Poor old horse, poor old horse.

So my skin unto the huntsman I will freely give
And my body to the hounds, my boys, I'd rather die than live
My poor old body sweet that's been so many a mile
Over hedges, over ditches, likewise gates and stiles
  Poor old horse, poor old horse

THE PRENTICE BOY (THE MILLER'S APPRENTICE)

HAM/2/8/20, James Elliott, Todber, Dorset, September 1905.

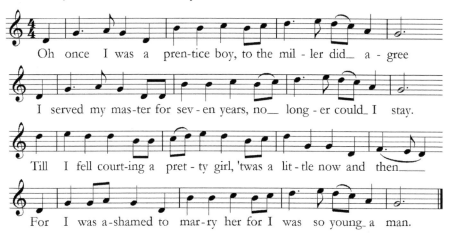

Oh once I was a prentice boy, to the miller did agree
I served my master for seven years, no longer could I stay
Till I fell courting a pretty girl, 'twas a little now and then
For I was ashamed to marry her for I was so young a man.

I went unto her sister's house at eight o'clock at night
And little did she think that I owed her any spite
I took her to the fields so green and to the meadows gay
And then we sat and talked a while for to fix the wedding day.

I took a stick all from the hedge, I laid her body down
Then the blood of innocence came pouring from the wound
When she on bended knees did fall and loud for mercy cry
Crying, Jimmy dear, don't murder me, for I'm not fit to die.

I took her by the curly locks, I dragged her through groves so green
Until I came to some river side and there I throwed her in
All with the blood of innocence my hands and clothes were dyed
Instead of being a pitiless corpse, oh she ought to have been my bride.

I went unto my master's house at twelve o'clock at night
He quickly came to let me in and he quickly struck a light
When the master begin for to question me what stain my hands and clothes
The answer that I had for him, 'twas the bleeding of my nose.

About nine weeks after, oh this pretty girl was found
Down the river floating clear not far from Ensmore town
When the judges and the jury they do so well agree
For the murdering of my own sweetheart, oh a-hanged I must be.

THE PRICKLY BUSH (THE MAID FREED FROM THE GALLOWS)

GG/1/9/502, Charles Chivers, Basingstoke, Hampshire. September 1906

O hangman stay your hand, and stay it for a while
I think I see my own dear father coming over yonder stile.
Oh have you brought me gold, oh have you brought me fee,
Or have you come to see me hung all on this gallows tree?
I have not brought thee gold, I have not brought thee fee
But I am come to see thee hung all on this gallows tree.

Chorus: *Oh the bush, the prickly bush, which pricked my heart full sore*
If I could get out of that prickly bush, I'd never get in him any more.

The above is then repeated, the question being directed next to the mother, then to the brother,
then the sister, all of whom answer as above. Finally, however:

O hangman stay your hand, and stay it for a while
I think I see my own true-love coming over yonder stile
Oh have you brought me gold, oh have you brought me fee,
Or have you come to see me hung all on this gallows tree?
I have now brought thee gold, I have now brought thee fee
I am not come to see thee hung all on this gallows tree.

Chorus: *Oh the bush, the prickly bush, which pricked my heart full sore*
Now I have got out of that prickly bush, I'll never get in him any more.

THE QUEEN OF THE MAY

HAM/4/21/14, Sam Dawe, Beaminster, Dorset, June 1906

Now the winter is over and summer is come
And the meadows they look pleasant and gay
I spied a fair maid and so sweetly sung she
And her cheeks wore the blossom of May.
I said, My fair maid, oh it's how come you here
In these meadows so soon in the morn?
Oh the maid she replied, For to gather some May
For the trees are all now in full bloom.

I said, My fair maid, oh shall I accompany you
In these meadows so pleasant and gay?
Oh the maid she replied, I would rather be excused
I'm afraid you will lead me astray.
Then I took hold of her lily-white hand
'Pon the green mossy banks we sat down
Then I planted a kiss on her sweet ruby lips
While the small birds were singing all round.

And when we arose, oh she gave me a smile
And she thanked me for what I had done
Then I planted a sprig in her snowy-white breast
And believe me, there never grows a thorn.
'Twas early next morning I made her my bride
That the people might have nothing to say
Then the bells they did ring and the bridesmaids did sing
And I crowned her the Queen of the May.

Robin Hood and the Tanner

GG/1/3/79, William Randall, Hursley, Hampshire, June 1905, with slight amendments from: GG/1/20/1221, James Buckland, Micheldever, Hampshire, September 1908.

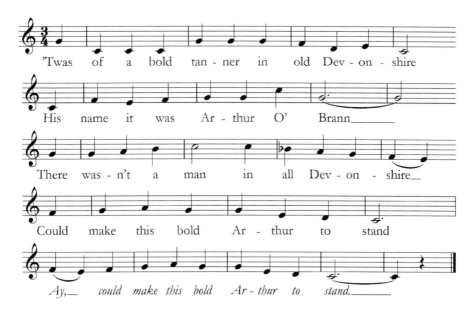

'Twas of a bold tanner in old Devonshire
His name it was Arthur O'Brann
There wasn't a man in all Devonshire
Could make this bold Arthur to stand
Ay, could make this bold Arthur to stand.

Bold Arthur walked out one fine summer's
  morn
To view the merry greenwood
In search of a deer that runs here and there
And there he spied bold Robin Hood
Ay, and there he spied bold Robin Hood.

Good morning, young fellow, says bold
  Robin Hood
What business hast thou here?
I will tell thee in brief, thou look'st like a
  thief
Thou art come for to steal the king's deer
Ay, thou art come for to steal the king's deer.

I will have a fat doe before I do go
Although it may cause me a fall
For I have a staff made out of green graft
And I think he would do for you all
Ay, and I think he would do for you all.

And I have another, says bold Robin Hood
Made out of the bonny oak tree
Three feet and a half, he will knock down a
  calf
And I think he would knock down thee
Ay, and I think he would knock down thee.

Let's measure our sticks, says bold Robin
  Hood
Before we commence our fray
If mine shall be half a foot longer than
  thine
Oh that shall be counted fair* play
Ay, and that shall be counted fair play.

They measured their sticks and at it they
  went
For the space of one hour or more
And every blow made the groves for to ring
They played their game so sure
Ay, they played their game so sure.

Hold on, hold on, says bold Robin Hood
I pray let our courage to fall
Before that we break our bones all to smash
And gain no coin at all
Ay, and gain no coin at all.

Bold Robin pulled out his long bugle horn
He blowed it so loud and so shrill
And then thereupon, he spied Little John
Come tripping down over the hill
Ay, come tripping down over the hill.

Oh what is the matter? then said Little
  John
I pray thee, bold Robin, me tell
There's something amiss, I'm sure that
  there is
For I see that thee doesn't look well
Ay, I see that thee doesn't look well

Oh, here I stand with my staff in my hand
Bold tanner he stands by my side
He's a bonny, brisk man, just fit for our
  gang
And so well he has tanned my hide
Ay, and so well he has tanned my hide.

Oh, if he's a tanner, then says Little John
A tanner that tans so true
There's not the least doubt he will have
  another bout
And so well he shall tan my hide too
Ay, and so well he shall tan my hide too.

Oh no, oh no, says bold Robin Hood
For he's a hero so bold
He's a bonny brisk blade and he's master of
  his trade
And by no man he won't be controlled
Ay, and by no man he won't be controlled.

** Mr Randall sang foul play, but most versions
agree that fair is right*

ROSEMARY LANE

HAM/2/7/13, William Bartlett in Wimborne Union, Dorset, 1905.

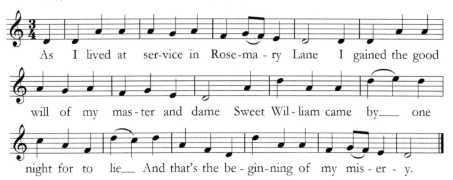

As I lived at service in Rosemary Lane
I gained the goodwill of my master and dame
Sweet William came by one night for to lie
And that's the beginning of my misery.

Now he called for a candle to light him to bed
Likewise a silk cap to tie round his head
For to tie round his head as he used to do
And he said, Pretty Nancy, will you come to bed too?

So poor little Nancy she thought it no harm
She jumped into bed for to keep herself warm
Oh what they done there they never will declare
But they wished that short night had been seven long year.

Oh early next morning sweet William arose
And into her bosom threw handfuls of gold
Oh this I will give you and more I will give
If you'll be my true-love as long as I live.

Oh if you have a baby, you put it out to nurse
And sit like a lady with gold in your purse
With gold in your purse and milk in your breast
Oh that's what you got from sweet William from the west.

Oh if it be a son it shall fight for the king
And if it be a daughter it shall wear a gold ring
It shall wear a gold ring and its top-knot shall blow
And that's what you got from sweet William, true blue.

THE ROVING BACHELOR

Tune and stanzas 1, 3, 5, 7 and 8 and refrain: GG/1/17/1089, William Bone, Medstead, Hampshire, November 1907, and stanzas 2, 4 and 6: HAM/2/3/5, Harry Conybeare, Combe Florey, Somerset, 1905.

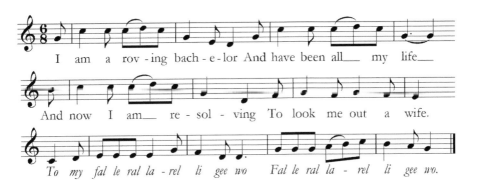

I am a roving bachelor
And have been all my life
And now I am resolving
To look me out a wife.

Chorus: *To my fal le ral larel li gee wo*
Fal le ral larel li gee wo.

Oh such a wife as I shall choose
She is not to be found
Oh such a wife as I shall choose
She is not on the ground.

If I should marry a young one
She'd kill me by her pride
If I should marry an old one
She'd lie grunting by my side.

If I should marry a tall one
She'd crack me on the crown
If I should marry a short one
She'd pull me to the ground.

If I should marry an ugly one
The boys would laugh at me
If I should marry a pretty one
A cuckoo I should be.

One night as I lay on my bed
How strange it came to pass
Who did I see by my bedside
But a handsome roving lass.

The first thing that I asked of her
If ever she were a maid
The answer that she gave to me
Oh yes, I am a maid.

The next thing that I asked of her
If ever she had a man
The answer that she gave to me
Oh yes, and when I can.

THE SAILOR'S TRAGEDY

Tune: HAM/4/22/22, Sam Gregory, Beaminster, Dorset, June 1906.
Text: parts of stanzas 1, 2 and 4, and the whole of stanzas 10 and 11, from HAM/4/22/22; stanzas 3, 5–9, 13, and 14 from GG/1/6/315, George Blake, St Denys, Southampton, Hampshire, June 1906; stanzas 12, 15, and 16 from HAM/5/26/37, from an old man in Marlborough Workhouse, Wiltshire, February, 1908.

It's of a sailor of whom I write
Who in the seas took great delight
Two maidens fair he did beguile
And both of them did prove with child.

He promised to be true to both
And bound them safe all with an oath
To marry them both it would cause strife
So one of them he made his wife.

The other, her public shame to prevent
Into a silent wood she went
And soon she ended up the strife
She cut the tender thread of life.

She hanged herself up to some tree
Where men a-hunting did her see
Her flesh by birds was beastly tore
Which grieved those young men's hearts
   full sore.

They took a knife and cut her down
And in her bosom a note was found
This note was written out in large
Bury me not I do you charge.

But here on earth then let me lie
That everyone that do pass by
They may by me a warning take
And shun their folly before 'tis too late.

Since he is false, then I'll be just
For here on earth he shall have no rest.
These words she said, they plagued him so
That to the seas he was forced to go.

One day while at the mainmast high
A little boat he chanced to spy
He was thinking on that wicked deed
Which almost made his heart to bleed.

Then down on deck this young man goes
And to the captain his mind disclosed.
Oh captain, stand in my defence
There's a spirit coming will fetch me hence.

The spirit all on the deck did stand
Enquiring for this wicked young man.
That young man, he died long ago
He died for the loss and love of you.

Captain, captain, how canst thou say so?
That young man is down in the hold below.
And if thou dost not bring him to me
Thy ship in a flame of fire shall be.

And if you stand in his defence
A mighty storm I will send hence
Which will make both you and your men
   to weep
And leave you sleeping in the deep.

Then down from the deck the captain goes
Brought up this young man to face his foes.
She fixed her eyes on him so grim
Which made him tremble in every limb.

It is well known when I was a maid
'Twas first by thee I was betrayed
I am a spirit sent for thou
You deceived me once, I'll have thee now.

Now to protect both ship and men
Into the boat they forced him then.
The boat sank in a flame of fire
Which made the seamen all admire.

Come all young men that to love belong
Be mindful of my mournful song.
Be true and faithful in your mind
And not delude poor womankind.

Seven Months I've Been Married

GG/1/21/1341, Frank Phillips, Stoney Cross, Hampshire, April 1909.

Seven months I've been married and all to my grief
Seven months I've been married but found no relief
Seven months I've been married but still I'm a maid
For I'm ruined, I'm ruined for ever, she said.

Oh he comes to bed to me, oh every night
He calls me his jewel and his sweet heart's delight
But the love that hangs on him is like the leaves on the trees
But I'm ruined, I'm ruined for ever, cried she.

Oh he brings me fine ribbons all decored with gold
And many a fine story to me he has told
But I would give them all for the sake of a man
But I'm ruined, I'm ruined, do all that I can.

My father he gave me eight acres of ground
My mother she gave me eight hundred pounds
But I will give them all for the sake of a man
I'm ruined, I'm ruined, do all that I can.

So it's come all you young maidens, take a warning by me
Never marry an old man in any degree
You marry a young man that will make you his wife
And then you'll live happy all the days of your life.

SEVENTEEN COME SUNDAY

Tune: GG/1/21/1351, John (or James) Brading, Alverstoke House of Industry, Hampshire, April 1908.
Text: GG/1/19/1203, James Hiscock, Bartley, Hampshire, September 1908.

As I walked out one May morning
One May morning so early
'Twas there I spied a fair pretty maid
Just as the sun was a-rising

Chorus: *With my ru rum day*
Fol the riddle day
Rite fal lal liddle li do.

Her stockings white, her shoes was bright
And her buckles shone like silver
She had a dark and a rolling eye
And her hair hung down her shoulder.

Where are you going, my fair pretty maid?
Where are you going, my honey?
She answered me very cheerfully
On an errand for my mammy.

How old are you, my fair pretty maid?
How old are you, my honey?
She answered me very cheerfully
I am seventeen come Sunday.

Will you take a man, my fair pretty maid?
Will you take a man, my honey?
She answered me very cheerfully
I dare not for my mammy.

Will you come down to my mammy's
house
When the moon shines bright and clearly?
I will come downstairs and let you in
And my mammy shall not hear me.

I went down to her mammy's house
When the moon shone bright and clearly
She came downstairs and she let me in
And I laid in her arms till morning.

Now soldier will you marry me?
Now is your time or never
For if you do not marry me
I am undone forever.

Now she is with her soldier bright
Where the wars they are alarming
A fife and drum is her delight
And a pint of rum in the morning.

SHEFFIELD PARK

Tune and Text: GG/1/5/274, Moses Blake, Emery Down, Lyndhurst, Hampshire, May 1906 with stanza 7
from: GG/1/16/1010, George Whiteland, Preston Candover, Alresford, Hampshire, October 1907.

In Shef-field Park,__ oh there did dwell A brisk young lad,__ I know him well. He court-ed me__ my heart to gain But he's gone and left__ me full of__ pain.

In Sheffield Park, oh there did dwell
A brisk young lad, I know him well.
He courted me my heart to gain
But he's gone and left me full of pain.

I went upstairs to make my bed
Laid myself down but nothing said
My mistress came to my bedside.
What is the matter with you, my maid?

O mistress, mistress, you little know
The pain and sorrow I undergo
Just clap your hand to my left breast
My aching heart can take no rest.

My mistress gone from my bedside
Some help, some help for you I'll find.
No help, no help, no help I crave
Sweet William has brought me to the
    grave.

It's take this letter immediately
And give it to him if he can read
Send me an answer without delay
For he think he stole my heart away.

He took the letter immediately
And read it while the maid sat by
Soon as he read it, the letter he burned
I take delight for to hear her mourn.

How could my love so foolish be
As to think I loves no one but she?
Man is not meant for one alone
I take delight for to hear her mourn.

A false young man I found thee art
It's thou that broke my young child's heart
In Abraham's bosom she shall sleep
Whilst thy tormenting soul doth weep.

They gathered green grass for her head
And a flowery pillow for her head
And the leaves that fall from tree to tree
Shall be the covering over she.

THE SHOPKEEPER

Tune: GG/1/9/499, Charles Chivers, Basingstoke, Hampshire, August 1906.
Text: mainly GG/1/16/1047 Mrs Knight, Hartley Wintney Workhouse, Hampshire. October 1907; minor
emendations from GG/1/9/499 and GG/1/14/851.

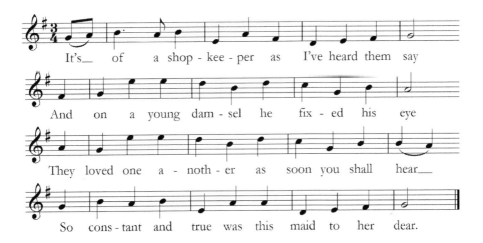

It's of a shopkeeper as I've heard them say
And on a young damsel he fixed his eye
They loved one another as soon you shall hear
So constant and true was this maid to her dear.

Her parents contrived to send her away
They sent her up to London and there for to stay
She hadn't been gone but a month and a day
Before she wrote her love a letter she was coming away.

Her love wrote back another, God send you long life
And when you return I will make you my wife
For what I do suffer no man shall ever know
For I will come to you whatsoever I go through.

There's one a-coming up and the other going down.
This damsel being a-tired she sat herself down.
She gave a long sigh and her tender heart did break
And she died on the road for her true-lover's sake.

This young man journeyed on till he came to an inn.
He called for a bottle to drink with his friend.
He says to the landlord, I'm a man from abroad,
Come, show me to the damsel that died on the road.

'Tis an heiress' corpse, the landlord did say
And when he came to her, he said, It is she.
It is my dearest jewel and the only one I crave
So let me and my true-love lie both in one grave.

Then dig us a grave, both long wide and deep
And a marble stone put at the head and the feet
And in the middle two true turtle-doves
To show all the world we died in true love.

SIX JOLLY MINERS

Tune and Text: GG/1/3/105, William Brown, Cheriton, Hampshire, 1905. Stanza 3 and slight amendments to text from: GG/1/20/1299, William Clark, Farringdon, Hampshire, October 1908.

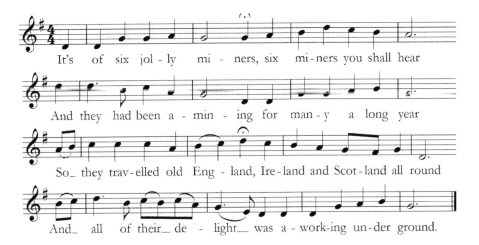

It's of six jolly miners, six miners you shall hear
And they had been a-mining for many a long year
So they travelled old England, Ireland, and Scotland all round
And all of their delight was a-working underground.

There was one came from Cornwall and two from Derby town
The other three from Williamsbridge, young lads of high renown
And all of their delight was to split those rocks in twain
And it's all for the treasure, my boys, as we do undermine.

The huntsman's delight is in blowing of his horn
And the farmer's delight is in housing of his corn
But all of our delight is to split those rocks in twain
And it's all for the treasure, my boys, as we do undermine.

Sometimes we have money, boys, sometimes we've none at all
But we can have good credit, my boys, when on it we do call.
We call for liquors merrily and drink our healths all round
Here's a health to all jolly miners that works all underground.

'Twas down by a crystal river stream I heard a fair maid sing*
Oh haven't you seen my miner? or hasn't he been this way?
Oh haven't you seen my miner? so sweetly sang she
For of all the trades in England it's the miner's for me.

*say?

THE SPOTTED COW

HAM/2/1/4, Amos Ash, Combe Florey, Somerset, April/May 1905.

One morn-ing in the month of May As from— my cot— I strayed

Just at the dawn-ing of— the day_ I met a charm-ing maid_

I met___ a charm - ing maid._____

One morning in the month of May
As from my cot I strayed
Just at the dawning of the day
I met a charming maid
I met a charming maid.

Good morning, fair maid! Whither, says I
So early? Tell me now.
The maid replied, Kind sir, she cried
I've lost my spotted cow
I've lost my spotted cow.

No more complain, no longer mourn
Your cow is not lost, my dear
I saw her down in yonder lawn
Come, love, I'll show you where
Come, love, I'll show you where.

I must confess you're very kind
I thank you, sir, said she
You will be sure she's there to find?
Come, sweetheart, go with me
Come, sweetheart, go with me.

Into the grove we did repair
Across the flowery dell
We hugged and kissed each other there
And love was all our tale
And love was all our tale.

Into the grove we spent the day
And thought it passed too soon.
At night we homeward bent our way
And brightly shone the moon
And brightly shone the moon.

If I should cross yon flowery dell
Or go to view the plough
She comes and calls her gentle swain
I've lost my spotted cow
I've lost my spotted cow.

T STANDS FOR THOMAS (THE FALSE YOUNG MAN)

Tune: GG/1/10/601, Alfred Porter, Basingstoke, Hampshire, November 1906.
Text: GG/1/10/601; stanza 2, lines 3–4, stanza 3, lines 1–2, and stanza 4 from Robert King, Castle Eaton, Wiltshire (Alfred Williams MS Collection, Wt 342).

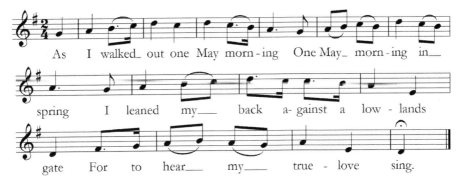

As I walked out one May morning One May morning in spring I leaned my back against a lowlands gate For to hear my true-love sing.

As I walked out one May morning
One May morning in spring
I leaned my back against a lowlands gate
For to hear my true-love sing.

For to hear my true-love sing a song
And to hear what she had to say
For I wished to know more of her mind
Before I went away.

Come sit you down all by my side
On the grass that grows so green
For it's more than three-quarters of one
    year
Since together you and I have been.

I never will believe what an old man does
    say
For his days they cannot be long
And I never will believe what the young
    men say
For they promise, but marry none.

There's T stands for Thomas, as I've heard
    them say
And J stands for my man John
And W it stands for my sweet William
But Johnny is the handsomest man.

I climbed up the top of the highest of the
    trees
And robbed the cuckoo of her nest
Then I'll return safe home again
And get married to the girl I love best.

TARRY TROUSERS

Tune: GG/1/16/993, Mrs Hall, Axford, Basingstoke, October 1907.
Text: GG/1/16/993; stanza 3 from GG/1/11/638, Benjamin Arnold, Easton, Winchester, November 1906.

As I walked out one midsummer morning
The weather being fine and clear
There I heard a tender mother
Talking to her daughter dear.

Says the mother, I would have you marry
And live no longer a single life.
Oh no, says she, I would sooner tarry
For my jolly sailor bright.

I know you would have me wed with a
        farmer
And not give me my heart's delight
Give me the lad with the tarry trousers
Shines to me like diamonds bright.

O daughter, sailors are given to roving
And to some foreign parts they go
Then they'll leave you broken-hearted
And they'll prove your overthrow.

Oh sailors they are men of honour
And do face their enemy
When the thundering cannons rattle
And the bullets they do fly.

Polly, my dear, our anchor is waiting*
And I am come to take my leave
Although I love you, my dear jewel
Charming Polly, do not grieve.

Jamie, my dear, let me go with you
No foreign dangers will I fear
When you are in the height of battle
I will attend on you, my dear.

Hark, oh hark, how the great guns do
        rattle
And the small guns do make a noise
When they are in the height of battle
She cries, Fight on, my jolly, jolly boys.

Now all pretty maidens pray give attention
If a jolly sailor is your delight
Never be forced to wed with another
For all their gold and silver bright.

weighing?

THREE JOLLY SNEAKSMEN

GG/1/13/826, Thomas Jones, Portsmouth Workhouse, Hampshire, August 1907.

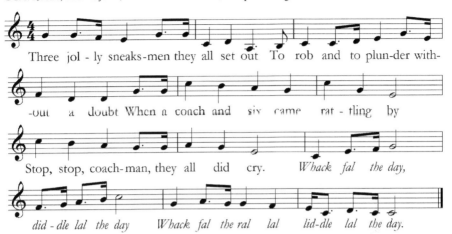

Three jolly sneaksmen they all set out
To rob and to plunder without a doubt
When a coach and six came rattling by
Stop, stop, coachman, they all did cry.

Chorus: *Whack fal the day, diddle lal the*
day
Whack fal the ral lal liddle lal the day.

As they stepped up into the coach
Three fair ladies did approach
They all cried out, What shall we do?
Deliver up your money and we won't hurt
you.

Five hundred pounds they paid in gold
Lord, 'twas a sight for to behold
A silver-headed sword and a gold lace cap
It was a fine haul for sneaksmen to snap.

As they were a-going up Hyde Park street
Three blue-coated gentlemen they
happened to meet
They tapped them on the shoulder, one,
two, three
Saying, My jolly little sneaksmen, you
must come along with me.

Our 'sizes and sessions is drawing near
And at the bar they did appear
When the judge cast round his rolling eye
Saying, My jolly little sneaksmen, you're
bound for to die.

As they went up the gallows tree
Jack Ketch was there as soon as they.
He took their togs and rino* too
Saying, Now to the world you must all bid
adieu.

money

TOM BARBARY (WILLIE O' WINSBURY)

Tune: GG/1/11/684, Charles Bull, Marchwood, Southampton, Hampshire, June 1907.
Text: GG/1/11/684; stanzas 7 and 11 from GG/1/20/1317, Fred Osman, Lower Bartley, Hampshire, November 1908.

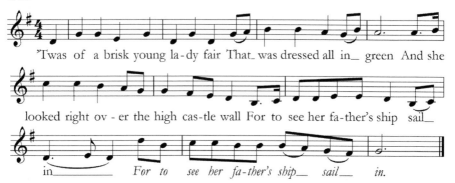

'Twas of a brisk young la-dy fair That was dressed all in green And she looked right ov-er the high cas-tle wall For to see her fa-ther's ship sail in For to see her fa-ther's ship sail in.

'Twas of a brisk young lady fair
That was dressed all in green
And she looked right over the high castle wall
For to see her father's ship sail in
For to see her father's ship sail in.

What is the matter with my daughter dear
She looks so pale and wan?
Have you been afflicted by any illness
Or been lying with a false young man
Or been lying with a false young man?

No, I have not been afflicted by any illness
Nor been lying with a false young man
For what does grieve me to the very, very heart
You've been staying so long from home
You've been staying so long from home.

Now pull off your gown of green
And lay it wide along.
And her very under-petticoat had grown so short before
She was full three quarters gone
She was full three quarters gone.

Is it by any lord or duke
Or by any gentleman
Or is it by any sea captain
That so lately's come to land
That so lately's come to land?

No, it's not by any sea captain
Nor by any gentleman
For it is by young Thomas, young Thomas so bright
Your honoured servant-man
Your honoured servant-man.

Well, and if it's by Tom Barbary
I think you're not to blame
For I really do believe if I'd been a maid myself
That I might have lain with him
That I might have lain with him

Now he called up his servant-men
By ones and twos and threes
And young Thomas who used to be the very, very first
The last came in was he
The last came in was he.

Now wilt thou wed my daughter dear
And take her by the hand?
For 'tis you that shall dine and shall sup along with me
And be heir over all my land
And be heir over all my land.

Yes, I will wed your daughter dear
And take her by the hand
And I will dine and will sup along with you
But a fig for all your land
But a fig for all your land.

For I am one of the king's own sons
From Dublin town I come
And where you may give her one penny
I can give her a thousand and one
I can give her a thousand and one.

For I've got gold and silver in store
I've got houses and land
If it had not been for your daughter, daughter dear
I should never have been your servant-man
I should never have been your servant-man.

THE UNFORTUNATE LASS (THE SAILOR CUT DOWN IN HIS PRIME)

Tune: GG/1/21/1431, Charles Shears, Salisbury Union, Wiltshire, August 1909.
Text: mainly GG/1/10/582, Henry Adams, Basingstoke, Hampshire, September 1906; slightly augmented from a broadside.

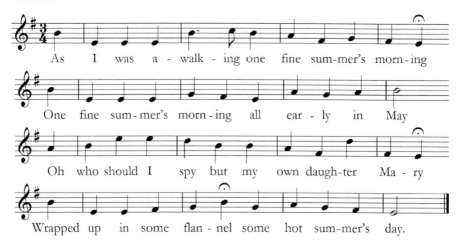

As I was a-walking one fine summer's morning
One fine summer's morning all early in May
Oh who should I spy but my own daughter Mary
Wrapped up in some flannel some hot summer's day.

O mother, o mother, come sit you down by me
Come sit you down by me and pity my case
It's of a young officer lately deserted
See how he has brought me to shame and disgrace.

O daughter, o daughter, why hadn't you told me
Why hadn't you told me, we'd took it in time
I might have got salts and pills of white mercury
But now I'm a young girl cut down in my prime.

O doctor, o doctor, come wash up your bottles
Come wash up your bottles and wipe them quite dry
My bones they are aching, my poor heart's a-breaking
And I in a deep solemn fashion must die.

Have six jolly fellows to carry my coffin
Have six pretty maidens to bear up my pall
Give to each pretty fair maid a glass of brown ale
Saying, Here lies the bones of a true-hearted girl.

Come rattle your drums and play your fifes merrily
Merrily play the dead marches along
And over my coffin throw handfuls of laurel
Saying, There goes a true-hearted girl to her home.

THE WANTON SEED

Tune and Text: HAM/3/17/5, J. Pomery (of Broad Oak) in Bridport Union, Dorset, May 1906. Text slightly augmented from a broadside by Bloomer of Birmingham.

As I walked out one morning fair
To view the fields and take the air
There I heard a pretty maid making her complaint
And all she wanted was the chiefest grain
Chiefest grain
And all she wanted was the chiefest grain.

I stepped up to this pretty maid
And unto her these words I said
I said, My pretty maid do you stand in need?
I've a grain that is called the wanton seed
Wanton seed, etc.

Oh yes, kind sir, I do stand in need
Of a grain that is called the wanton seed
And if you are the man who can do the deed
Come and sow my meadow with the wanton seed
Wanton seed, etc.

Then I sowed high and I sowed low
And under her apron the seed did grow.
It sprung up so neatly without any weed
And she always commended my wanton seed
Wanton seed, etc.

When forty weeks was gone and past
She came unto me with a slender waist.
She came unto me making this complaint
That she wanted some more of the chiefest grain
Chiefest grain, etc.

WATERCRESSES

GG/1/7/402, George Lovett, Winchester, Hampshire, August 1906.

I am a jolly farmer, from Bedfordshire I came
To see some friends at Camberwell and Morgan is my name
At a dairy farm near Dunstable I live when I'm at home
And if I gets safe back again, from there I'll never roam.
But if you'll pay attention, I'll tell without delay
How a buxom little damsel my affections led astray
She promised for to marry me all on the first of May
And she left me with a bunch of watercresses.

I politely addressed her and thus to her did say
I wish to go to Camberwell, can you direct the way?
Oh yes, sir, oh yes, sir, she speedily replied
Take the turning on your left, then go down the other side.
Her voice it was the sweetest I ever yet did hear
In her hands which like the lilies were so very white and clear
She had a bunch of early onions and half a pint of beer
Some pickles and a bunch of watercresses.

I bowed and I thanked her and we walked side by side
I thought how well she'd like to be a dairy farmer's bride.
I gathered resolution, half in earnest, half in joke
I hinted matrimony, those very words I spoke
I've a farm of forty acres, I've horses, cows and geese
Besides I have a dairy filled with butter, milk and cheese
Will you marry me and mistress be, fair lady, all of these?
And we'll pass our days in love and watercresses.

She replied with a smile, or a leer if you choose
Dear sir, you are so very generous, I cannot well refuse
Pray give me your direction, I will without delay
Prepare for matrimony, love, honour and obey
I've a wedding dress to buy, and some little bills to pay.
I handed her a sovereign, expenses to defray
When she promised for to marry me all on the first of May
And she left me with a bunch of watercresses.

Next day a letter I received, I read there with surprise
Dear sir, for disappointing you I must apologise
But when next you ask a stranger into partnership for life
Be sure she's a maiden or a widow, not a wife
I've a husband of my own and his name is Willie Gray
And when I can afford it, your sovereign I will pay
To think that I should marry you all on the first of May!
Why, you must have been as green as watercresses!

YOUNG JOHNNY WAS A PLOUGHBOY (YOUNG ROGER THE PLOUGHBOY)

GG/1/5/280, Moses Blake, Emery Down, Lyndhurst, Hampshire, June 1906.

Young Johnny was a ploughboy, a crafty young swain
He went whistling and singing all over the plain
Till he met with black-eyed Susan and her maidenhead
And he valued her much more than the hairs on his head.

Good morning, pretty fair maid, you are in good time
There's one thing I ask you, I think it no crime
Will you go along with me, my love, tomorrow to the fair?
I will buy you some ribbons for to roll in your hair.

The girl seemed uneasy, not willing for to go
I wants no young man's ribbons, I would have you to know
So don't trouble me nor tease me, it's more than you dare
I wants no young man's ribbons for to roll in my hair.

As they walked along together down by some shady grove
Where no one could see them but the angels above
There he laid her down so softly before she was aware
And he gave her some ribbons to roll in her hair.

When young girls are breeding they looks both pale and wan
And all they want to do is to please their young man
So be constant and true-hearted wherever that you are
You shall never want for ribbons to roll in your hair.

YOUNG JOHNSON

Tune: GG/1/5/230, James Rampton, Whitchurch, Hampshire, May 1906.
Text: stanza 1, first half of stanza 2, and second half of stanza 3 from GG/1/5/230; completed from a broadside by Ryle of Seven Dials, final stanza amended from a broadside by Marshall of Newcastle.

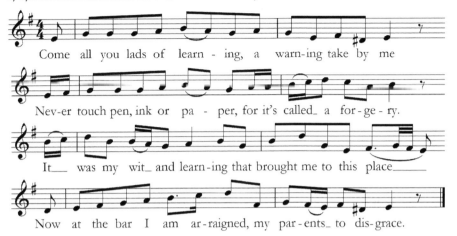

Come all you lads of learning, a warning take by me
Never touch pen, ink or paper, for it's called a forgery
It was my wit and learning that brought me to this place
Now at the bar I am arraigned, my parents to disgrace.

Young Johnson being a clever lad, well dressed from top to toe
When the judge condemned him for to die, tears from his eyes did flow
The neighbours that around him stood one thousand pounds would give
All for the life of Johnson if they would him reprieve.

Then up starts the jury, Oh no, that must not be
If you would give ten thousand pounds we could not let him go free
For his uncle he is standing by all with the forged will
We are forced to hang young Johnson though much against our will.

As Johnson rode up Holborn Hill so mildly then spake he
Saying, I freely forgive them if they will forgive me.
Then with a smiling countenance he made a graceful bow
Farewell, farewell, to this vain world I now must bid adieu.

Notes on the Songs

Song Titles

Main titles are mostly those of the singers but some are Purslow's editorial titles. Those in brackets are from Steve Gardham's Master Titles Index, which in cooperation with the Roud Index selects the most commonly used title from published collections. It is a testament to the influence of this series of books that most of the first edition titles have actually become Master Titles.

Abroad as I Was Walking (The Distressed Maid)

Roud 564 (Laws P 18)

Known as 'The Distressed Maid' on broadsides (e.g. Bodleian Library, *Harding B15 (220b)*), this ballad has become crossed with another broadside ballad, 'The Dublin Tragedy' (see 'Molly and William' in this book), during the twentieth century. Alfred Porter's text is mostly of the former, but the hybrid text, made up of a condensed version of the former with the ending of the latter, has become widespread in England, usually under the title 'The Lily-White Hand'. In the hybrid form, the girl is drowned by her lover, who then regrets his actions (see GG/1/18/1145).

For Porter's text and further versions of 'The Distressed Maid', see GG/1/10/589, GG/1/13/781, GG/1/20/1318, GG/1/21/1397, HAM/3/11/23, HAM/3/18/2, HAM/4/30/2, HAM/4/30/20. Stanza 6 in this book is a composite of GG/1/10/589 and GG/1/13/781. A much earlier version of the ballad, 'The Forsaken Damosel; or, The Deluded Maid' (c.1670) is at Bodleian Library, Rawlinson Ballads 566 (24). A more detailed history is at <www.mustrad.org.uk/articles/dung19.htm>.

Versions from tradition: Topic TSCD660, *Who's that at my bed window?* (Paddy Tunney, Donegal, 'Blackwaterside'); Topic TSCD512D, *The Bonny Labouring Boy,* (Harry Cox, Norfolk, 'The Grand Hotel'); Musical Traditions MTCD345 *The Brazil Family: Down by the Old Riverside* (Harry Brazil, Doris Davies, Danny and Lemmie Brazil, 'The Old Riverside'); Veteran VT119 *Catch Me if You Can* (Sophie Legg, Cornwall, 'Down by the Old Riverside'); Veteran VTD148CD *A Shropshire Lad* (Fred Jordan, Shropshire, 'Down by the Riverside'); British Library, Archival Sound Recordings, Traditional Music in England 1CDR0010643 C1009/18 (William Henry Reed, Yorkshire, 'The Watery Grave'); Topic TSCD672D *I'm a Romany Rai* (Rebecca Penfold, Devon, 'Meeting is a Pleasant Place').

All through the Beer (Good Brown Ale and Tobacco)
Roud 475

Purslow collated Charles Chivers's defective chorus with a version noted by Alfred Williams in Oxfordshire (Alfred Williams MS Collection, Ox 287). Chivers's chorus started 'Then he shouted out hurrah for his grog and tobacco', which links his version up to those titled 'All for me Grog'. Accordingly, Purslow has reconstructed the tune at bars 13 and 14 to accommodate the Oxfordshire chorus. The only other notable alteration to the text he made is in the fourth stanza where he gave in brackets the word 'seat', and it doesn't take much imagination to guess Chivers's actual word. Chivers's title was 'The Nobby Hat'.

The earliest extant version, 'If e'er I do well, 'tis a wonder', was printed in Allan Ramsay's *Tea-Table Miscellany* (1740), pp. 357–59, but there is nothing to suggest that it originated there, or indeed that it had any Scottish connection. The chorus is given as 'Fall all de rall, &c.' This version also appeared in Johnson's *Scots Musical Museum* (1787–1803), no. 322, with chorus and tune. Here, all his money is spent not on beer or grog but on whores, bawds, and queans. A version called 'This Old Coat of Mine' was very popular with British forces' Sods' Operas during the Second World War, accompanied by the stripping-down actions often found with earlier bar-room versions. As 'All For Me Grog' it entered a new phase of life in the 1950s folk revival, and is still popular today.

Versions from tradition: Topic TSCD663 *They ordered their pints of beer and bottles of sherry* (Tom Newman, Oxfordshire, 'My Old Hat that I Got On'); Musical Traditions MTCD306 *Put a Bit of Powder on it, Father* (Walter Pardon, Norfolk, 'Here's to the Grog'); Helions Bumpstead NLCD5 *Voice of Suffolk* (George Cowle, Suffolk, 'We'll Call for the Grog').

All under the New-Mown Hay
Roud 7180

Purslow introduced his note on this song: 'This is presumably the landlubbers' song from which the well-known shanty "A-Roving" developed…' Although the landlubbers' song is much rarer, he presumed correctly. The few widespread versions that do exist clearly demonstrate the evolution from land song to sea song, as is often the case with shanties, although we have not been able to trace an original or a broadside. Three fragmentary versions were found in north-east Scotland, given under the umbrella title of 'Ye Wanton Young Women' in the *Greig–Duncan Folk Song Collection*, ed. by Patrick Shuldham-Shaw, Emily B. Lyle, et al., 8 vols (Aberdeen: Aberdeen University Press; Edinburgh: Mercat Press, 1981–2002), II, 397–98. Sharp collected a fragment in Somerset called 'We'll go no more a-cruising' (Sharp MSS, Folk Words 529). The fragment collected by Annie Gilchrist at Southport, 'I'll go no more a-roving', is the clincher, being just halfway between land song and sea song (JFSS, 2.4 (no. 9) (1906), 245). The oft-repeated assertion that these songs derive from a catch in Thomas Heywood's play *The Rape of Lucrece* is nonsense; all they have in common is the much-used bawdy theme found in many songs and a few versions of the shanty.

Modern version (based on this one): Topic TSCD492 *Skin and Bone* (Martin Carthy and Dave Swarbrick, 'The New Mown Hay').

The Barley Raking
Roud 1024

There is some confusion over the source cited here (GG/1/16/989). On the manuscript music notation Mrs Hall of Axford is credited, but the fragment of text is attributed to Mrs Randall of Preston Candover. Purslow has collated the first stanza and chorus from Mrs Randall and Henry Godwin. Henry Godwin's chorus was three lines of vocables followed by 'Remember the barley raking' (GG/1/3/80).

Purslow amended stanza 3 and added stanza 4 from a Fortey broadside. These broadside versions were widely printed in the early nineteenth century and even the earliest have quite garbled texts, suggesting the influence of oral tradition and, furthermore, that the original was of at least the mid-eighteenth century. Purslow stated that the tune is an old jig called 'Merrily Danced the Quaker's Wife', but it is much closer to the Kirkby Malzeard sword dance tune 'Lass o' Dallowgill'.

Bedlam (Through Moorfields)
Roud 605

Text and tune are from Moses Blake, Emery Down, Lyndhurst, Hampshire, who had the first two stanzas and two other stanzas made up of bits from the remaining four, of which the missing parts are supplied by a Disley of London broadside. Bedlam, or the Old Bethlehem Hospital, stood in Moorfields, London, from 1675 until 1814. This is one of many female laments set therein, but most of them lack the happy ending seen here. The ballad appeared under various titles in eighteenth century garlands and even these show variety in text and length which would suggest it originated earlier in the century rather than later and was probably from some theatrical production. There were many titles for this ballad on broadsides. Guyer and Gardiner's preferred title was 'Moorfields' and Purslow's editorial title is unfortunate as this is easily confused with many others on the same subject. In JFSS Volume 1, Number 4, 1902, Part 1, p146 Henry Burstow's fuller version is titled 'Through Moorfields' which I find less confusing. The tune given here is a common one much in use for broadside ballads of the same period. It was noted for Gardiner by Mr Guyer and judging by the half dozen attempts in the manuscripts at scoring it correctly they both had problems with the time signature, sometimes given as 4:2.

For a modern recording of Blake's version see: Forest Tracks FTBT2CD1-H *Folk Songs from Hampshire* (Cheryl Jordan, Hampshire, track 3).

The Bed-making
Roud 1631

The tune is a variant of the well-known traditional 'Cuckoo's Nest' and is from the celebrated Mrs Marina Russell of Upwey, Dorset, who had many fine and unusual tunes. Oral versions are quite rare, found only in the English southern counties. Broadsides from the early nineteenth century were printed in London and the Midlands. Pitts, Catnach, and Birt (all of London) and their successors printed pretty much the same text under the title 'The Gay Old Man', with the following eighth stanza:

Come all you maids where'er you be,
Make your beds while you can see,
For I made mine by candlelight,
Which caus'd me to rue all the days of my life.

Not without interest here is a seventeenth-century broadside *The Skilfull Doctor of Gloucester-shire; or, A New Way to Take Physick*, which likewise tells the story of a maid got with child by her master (Pepys Ballads 1.531). The designated tune is 'The Beds Making'. Unfortunately, 'The Beds Making' has not survived (unless it is our song given here), but references to it date back to 1629. See Claude L. Simpson, *The British Broadside Ballad and its Music* (New Brunswick, NJ: Rutgers University Press, 1966), pp. 189–90 n. 2, and p. 752 n. 3, where it is noted as a lost tune. Another seventeenth century ballad, however, *A Woman's Work Is Never Done*, is set 'To a delicate Northern Tune, A Woman's Work Is Never Done; or, The Beds Making' (Roxburghe Ballads 1.534–535). In this housewife's complaint, which is assumed to be the original, the bed-making is literal, without any sexual activity implied, as shown by the first two lines of stanza 9: 'In making of the beds such pains I take, / Until my back, and sides, and arms, do ake'. The Roxburghe copy was printed by John Andrews at the White Lion in Pye-Corner, c.1655–60, but a copy was entered in the Stationers' Register in 1629.

Modern version based on Mrs Russell's: Topic TSCD300, *Crown of Horn* (Martin Carthy).

Betsy the Serving Maid (Betsy the Servant Maid)
Roud 156

Though not a common ballad in oral tradition, 'Betsy the Serving Maid' is certainly widespread. This is not surprising since it had been printed on broadsides in one form or another for at least two centuries before being noted down by collectors. The great Norfolk singer Harry Cox made the ballad famous and he claimed in the 1950s that it had been sung in his family for two centuries. It appears to have remained strong in oral tradition and some stanzas still commonly sung today are not found on extant broadsides printed after 1700.

The nineteen-stanza version titled *Pretty Betty*, printed in Newcastle by Angus, c.1800 (Robert White Collection 20.58), appears to be a rewritten version using material from two ballads printed in London by Charles Barnet, c.1690–1700: *Constancy Lamented; or, A Warning for Unkind Parents* (Pepys Ballads 5.353) and *Love Overthrown. The Young Man's Misery, and The Maid's Ruine* (Pepys Ballads 5.305, 5.307). These ballads purport to be based on actual events, the preamble to Constancy Lamented summarizing the story as follows:

a full and true Account of a Wealthy Tradesman's Son in the Strand, who died on Friday last, for the Grief he conceived in the Absence of his dearly beloved E. H—ks (*a Hereford-shire Damsel*) who was by his Hard-hearted Mother, sold to Virginia; and of the many Arguments the Mother used to perswade this Young-Man to fix his love on some more Wealthy Maiden: With the Mothers sad lamentation, and almost Raving Distraction for her Son's Death, and her own most Unworthy Action. *The whole Published from the Relation of a Worthy young*

Gentlewoman, a daily Visitant of the said young Man's, and a sorrowful mourner for his great mishap.

Robert Barrett's version here is clearly derived from the twelve-stanza version printed by Pitts and others in London, c.1820.

Versions from tradition: Topic TSCD512D *The Bonny Labouring Boy* (Harry Cox, Norfolk, 'The Servant Maid').

Better for Maids to Live Single
Roud 1632
No other versions of this song are known. The subject is a popular one on broadsides and has been so for at least three centuries, addressed from the perspective of both sexes. It would appear that in song the topic of unhappy marriage has always been much more popular than the happy variety, whether treated seriously or humorously. The tune is typical of nineteenth-century stage Irish pieces, being related to 'Tread on the Tail of me Coat; or, Mush Mush', but it is also similar to the tune used for the Royal Earsdon sword dance calling-on song.

Purslow improved the tune in bars 11 and 12, since the notation did not make musical sense.

Blow the Candle Out
Roud 368 (Laws P 17)
Whilst this well-known song can hardly be termed popular in oral tradition over the last century, it is certainly widespread and has lasted, with the help of broadside printings, for at least three centuries. The text given here is easily recognizable as similar to that given by D'Urfey in *Pills to Purge Melancholy* (1719–20), VI, 342–43, but there is much to suggest that several rewritings for broadsides went on in the early nineteenth century; indeed, the prolific John Morgan, the most celebrated broadside writer of this period, wrote a popular parody called 'Blow the Candle In'. The main difference between D'Urfey's version and those of a century later is that his seven-stanza dialogue all takes place in the bedroom, whereas the later versions include the resulting pregnancy and the inevitable lament. As would be expected with dialogues of this sort, the order of stanzas varies somewhat from one version to another.

The tune is a variant of 'The Wearing of the Green', but more specifically is close to that used for 'I wish they'd do it now'. It bears no relation to any of the early tunes, or to the well-known minor tune.

Versions from tradition: Topic 12T158 [Rounder CD1778] The Folk Songs of Britain, vol. 2: *Songs of Seduction* (Jimmy Galhaney, Belfast); Topic TSCD660 *Who's that at my bed window?* (Jumbo Brightwell, Suffolk); Musical Traditions MTCD339 *A Story to Tell* (Jumbo Brightwell, Suffolk). Modern version: FTRAX 219 *Bottoms Up, Songs Miss Pringle Never Taught Us* (Frank Purslow and John Pearse).

The Blue Cockade (The White Cockade)
Roud 191

Although widely spread in Britain, this song does not appear to have travelled across the Atlantic – which is perhaps surprising considering the number of military campaigns in North America in its heyday. Late eighteenth-century printings vary enough to suggest an origin much earlier in the century. There are early versions set in both Scotland and Ireland, but it is pointless trying to pinpoint where it originated because regiments were relocated on a regular basis. The different coloured cockades – black, blue, white, orange, green, yellow, etc. – were worn on soldiers' hats to denote their regiment.

The tune seems to have been remarkably constant in all areas, although it is sometimes sung at a much livelier pace in north-east England. According to Purslow, it is an adaptation in common time of a triple-time tune called 'Love Will Find Out the Way' or 'Over the Mountains'.

Purslow patched together this new version from six out of eight versions collected by Hammond and Gardiner, almost like a jigsaw puzzle, half a stanza here, half a stanza there. Edwin Bugler contributes two and a half stanzas, Mrs Gulliver two, Richard Moore one, and another three half a stanza each. Tune and part text from Edwin Bugler (HAM/4/22/1) augmented with texts from Mrs Jane Gulliver (HAM/2/2/9), Richard Moore (GG/1/18/1126), David Clements (GG/1/9/538), David Marlow, Basingstoke, Hampshire, September 1906 (GG/1/10/564), and James Pike, Portsmouth Workhouse, Hampshire, August 1907 (GG/1/14/844).

Versions from tradition: British Library, Archival Sound Recordings, Traditional Music in England, 1CDR0009330 C1009/7 (Fred Jordan, Shropshire, 'The White Cockade'); FTRAX 518 *The White Cockade* (Keld Singers, Yorkshire, 'The White Cockade').

The Boatswain and the Tailor
Roud 570 (Laws Q 8)

Broadside versions of twelve stanzas, printed in London and elsewhere in the early nineteenth century, call this ballad *The Bold Boatswain of Dover* (e.g. Bodleian Library, Firth c.13(208)). W. Armstrong of Liverpool's nine-stanza version, *Ship in a Box*, however, sets the story in Liverpool (Bodleian Library, Harding B 28(259)). These differences are more likely to be attributable to rewriting than to oral tradition. The tune appears to be a variant of that used for a similar ballad, 'The Cunning Cobbler' (*Roud 174*), printed by Purslow in *The Constant Lovers* as 'The Cobbler and the Butcher'.

Versions from tradition:
<http://maxhunter.missouristate.edu/songinformation.aspx?ID=351>
Max Hunter Collection, 0351 (MFH 323) (Mrs Pearl Brewer, Arkansas, 'Johnny's Gone to Sea').

The Bold Dragoon
Roud 321 (Laws M27)

This version of the ballad, like almost all English oral versions, derives directly from the widely printed nineteenth-century English broadsides, with the same six stanzas but under a variety of titles whereby the dragoon can be 'jolly', 'bold', 'valiant', 'light', or just simply a 'dragoon'. All but the last stanza of these broadsides derive from *The Masterpiece of Love Songs*, in sixteen stanzas, c.1685 (Pepys Ballads 2.249), which in turn appears to derive from the slightly earlier *The Seaman's Renown in Winning his Fair Lady*, of twenty stanzas (Roxburghe Ballads 3.120–121, 4.72). *The Masterpiece of Love Songs* continued to be printed into the eighteenth century. The designated tune for both of these early ballads was the well-known 'The Week before Easter'. Both follow an *aaab* rhyming pattern. However, by the nineteenth century 'The Bold Dragoon' was beginning to run *abab*, until in oral tradition in the twentieth century all but two stanzas ran *abab*. It is quite likely that, as often happened, a broadside writer took a few stanzas from the longer ballad, crystallized the new one to meet the nineteenth-century fashion for shorter pieces, and tacked a typical moralizing 'come-all-ye' on to the end. However, at least two English, and most American, oral versions show some evidence of harking back to the longer ballads, so there could have been a slightly longer, eighteenth-century version in the interim.

It has often been suggested that this ballad has some details in common with 'Earl Brand' (*Child 7*) – the maid's request to the dragoon to stay his hand and spare one or more of his assailants, for example – but which came first is anyone's guess. It is likely that 'Earl Brand' has been influenced in some way by the broadsides.

Purslow printed stanza 4 from Mrs Hopkins in a slightly inaccurate form and without attribution. It is given here as it appears in Mrs Hopkins's text, where line 3 in the manuscript reads: 'So the dragoon drawed his (sword) cutlass which made the bones to rattle', with a note to put the word 'sword' in brackets.

Versions from tradition: Topic TSCD668 *To catch a fine buck was my delight* (Harry Brazil, Gloucester, 'Bold Keeper'); Musical Traditions MTCD346 *The Brazil Family: Down by the Old Riverside* (Danny Brazil and Harry Brazil, Gloucester, 'Bold Keeper'); Topic TSCD671 *You Never Heard So Sweet* (Enos White, Hampshire, 'The Bold Dragoon').

Bonny Kate
Roud 1633
There are only two other versions of this song, one from Sussex in the Clive Carey MSS (VWML, Sx186; Ms DM60), and the other from Devon in the Sharp MSS (Folk Tunes 487; Folk Words 582–583), although the story is a common one and there are plenty more bonny Kates and outwitted lawyers. The tune is rather unusual, not a typical folk tune, but more akin to the art songs of the eighteenth-century pleasure gardens.

Modern recording of William Burgess's version: Harvest CDEMS1477 *Anthems in Eden* (Shirley Collins).

The Boy and the Highwayman (The Crafty Ploughboy)
Roud 2637 (Laws L1)
The most common title for this well-known ballad is 'The Crafty Ploughboy'. It is one of a family of three ballads, the other two being 'The Highwayman Outwitted' (*Roud 2638; Laws L2*), in which a farmer's daughter is the heroine, and 'The Crafty Farmer' (*Roud 2640; Child 283*), in which a farmer gets the better of a highwayman. It is quite likely that all three were penned at about the same time, though Professor Child only selected one to

be honoured by inclusion in his great work *The English and Scottish Popular Ballads*. None of them has been traced back any further than c.1780, and all three were widely printed on broadsides, in many cases all three by the same printer.

The common plot is that, while the robber is picking up the victim's meagre earnings from the market, which s/he has deliberately scattered on the ground, the intended victim rides off on the highwayman's horse with all of his ill-gotten gains. In our ballad here, although the location varies from version to version, the boy is always from Yorkshire – a 'Yorkshire bite' being synonymous with a shrewd trick. Yorkshire folk are fabled for driving a hard bargain and having the ability to pull a fast one.

Versions from tradition: Musical Traditions MTCD345 *The Brazil Family; Down by the Old Riverside* (Danny Brazil, Gloucester, 'Jack and the Robber'); Veteran VT132 *From Donegal and Back* (Packie Byrne, Donegal, 'The Highwayman'); Topic 12TS257 *Songs of a Donegal Man* (Packie Byrne, Donegal, 'John and the Farmer'); Topic TSCD673T *Good People, Take Warning* (Bess Cronin, Co. Cork, 'Well Sold the Cow').

Modern recording of George Vincent's version: Forest Tracks FTBT 2CD1-D *Folk Songs from Dorset* (Steve Jordan).

Bright Phoebus
Roud 1634
Composed by James Hook in 1797, this is one of the great popular art songs from the last few years of the eighteenth century. So popular was it on both sides of the Atlantic that we should not be surprised to find it still being sung in the early years of the twentieth century. It is typical of the flowery hunting songs of the period and would have been quickly accepted into the hunt-supper repertoire, along with more earthy local pieces. Almost every phrase can be found in numerous similar songs of the period. Its transition from art song to street song would have been rapid, since it was printed on broadsides by the likes of Catnach and Pitts in London. Henry Brown's tune is recognizable as Hook's but lacking his repeats and a great many of his passing notes.

The Broken-Down Gentleman
Roud 383
Stanza 8 is unique to Blake's version, others having no more than eight stanzas and a fairly standard text as typified by Alfred Williams's Upper Thames version (*Folk Songs of the Upper Thames*, p87) and Grainger's North Lincolnshire version (*Yellowbelly Ballads*, O'Shaughnessy, p16). Harry Clifton wrote a more general song on exactly the same theme in the 1860s with the simpler title 'Broken Down'. The tune is quite consistent through all versions which might suggest a theatrical origin from some late eighteenth century musical play. About half of the versions have a repeat of the fourth line.

A Modern recording of Blake's version can be heard on Forest Tracks FTCD209 *George Blake's Legacy* (Tim Radford, Hampshire, track 5). For other recordings from the tradition see: Musical Traditions MTCD312 *Up in the North and Down in the South* (Bill Whiting, Berkshire, track 12), and Topic TSCD671 *You Never Heard So Sweet* (George Attrill, Sussex, track 15, 'The Broken-Down Gentleman').

Buttercup Joe
Roud 1635

A broadside by Pearson of Manchester states this song was sung by Harry Garratt, the favourite comic, though we have failed so far to discover sheet music or any further information on Garratt. The broadside's stock number is 657 and Pearson's sheets with similar stock numbers contain songs by Arthur Lloyd, which are more easily dated, to 1866 and 1873. The words appeared in the *National Prize Medal Song Book* in 1872.

The song went through a period of revival in the 1920s, when it was recorded by Albert Richardson in Sussex dialect, and in consequence this version has turned up in oral tradition ever since. For an excellent article on Richardson and the songs he popularized, see George Frampton, '"…and they calls I Buttercup Joe": Albert Richardson, the Singing Sexton of Burwash, 1905–76', FMJ, 9.2 (2007), 149–69. Its great popularity led to it being adapted as a 'yokel' piece in other parts of the country. I have recorded one such piece in Yorkshire <www.yorkshirefolksong.net> TYG 28, 'A Country Life For Me'.

Versions from tradition: Forest Tracks FTC6025 *Let this Room Be Cheerful* (Bob Mills, Hampshire); Musical Traditions MTCD310 *Just Another Saturday Night, Sussex 1960* (Jim Wilson, Sussex); Topic SP104 *Why Can't It Always Be Saturday?* (Harry Upton, Sussex); Zonophone 78 rpm disc TS5178 (Albert Richardson, Sussex).

The Buxom Lass (The Mower)
Roud 833

This song is a remake of an earlier ballad, 'The Mower'. Both existed contemporaneously as broadsides and both were frequently printed by the same printer. 'The Mower' can be found in several oral collections, but M. Hooper's version appears to be the only oral version of the later song. It is tempting to speculate that Hooper learned it directly from the broadside, as there is very little difference between his version and the Jackson of Birmingham broadside. The main distinction is that Hooper's song is narrated in the first person, whereas all the broadsides are in the third person after the first stanza. Purslow has substituted the sixth stanza from the broadside for Hooper's garbled stanza, which lacked the first line.

The extended sexual metaphor is typical of many late eighteenth-century pieces that use topographical features to describe human anatomy. As here, they sometimes comprise the entire *raison d'être* for the song. A sister ballad to this is 'The Little Farm; or, The Weary Ploughman' (*The Common Muse*, p452). The pattern and theme are exactly the same except that the narrator's occupation is that of ploughman rather than mower.

Modern versions: Fellside FECD87 *Voices: English Traditional Songs* (A. L. Lloyd, 'The Mower').

Captain Ward (Captain Ward and the Rainbow)
Roud 224 (Child 287)

For nigh on four centuries this ballad has remained popular both on broadsides and in oral tradition. Based on real events, ballads on Ward's exploits date from 1609, when the first one was entered in the Stationers' Register. Our ballad here was issued by several printers in the seventeenth century, the earliest being Francis Coles who was printing in the 1620s.

This twelve-stanza version continued to be printed on broadsides right up to Pitts's time, in the early nineteenth century. A version printed in Scotland, and later in the USA, has a few extra stanzas.

Gardiner had two other versions from Hampshire. As one might expect, the oral versions Gardiner collected all appear to derive from the condensed, eight-stanza version printed by Such of London and others in the mid-nineteenth century. In stanzas 3 and 6, Isaac Hobbes's and the other versions follow the broadside and have 'queen' instead of 'king'. By printing 'king', Purslow has restored the original reference to James I.

Versions from tradition: Musical Traditions MTCD303 *Plenty of Thyme* (Cyril Poacher, Suffolk, 'Captain Ward and the Rainbow').

Catch-Me-if-You-Can
Roud 1028
A scarce song on broadsides and in oral tradition: the sole extant broadside is *The Recreation* printed by Pitts of London (Madden Ballads, vol. 8 (London Printers, vol. 2), no. 1197), which is set out in six six-line stanzas, each equivalent to two stanzas in our oral version. (A song with the same title as the Pitts broadside was also listed in the catalogue of Collard of Bristol.) In the broadside, instead of going off to the wars, the villain has 'gone for recreation'. The 'horse and man' of stanza 9 is a corruption of the 'bold extortion man' of the broadside, presumably someone whose calling was to exact redress from the wayward (perhaps an early version of the Child Support Agency!). The Pitts ballad was printed at his 14 Great St Andrew Street address, which dates it before 1819.

The only published tunes come from the Hammond collection. It appears that the tune we hear in today's folk clubs is not the same as Marina Russell's. Hammond collected another tune from Jane Gulliver of Somerset, which is close to that sung by the Legg family of Travellers from Bodmin, Cornwall.

Versions from tradition: Veteran VT119 *Catch Me if You Can* (Sophie Legg, Cornwall).

Modern recording partly based on William Farnham's text: Wild Goose WGS340CD *Fenlandia* (Mary Humphreys, 'The Cuckoo and the Nightingale').

The Cluster of Nuts
Roud 1261
Although relatively scarce on broadsides and in oral tradition, this ballad was printed in England, Scotland, and Ireland, so it is not surprising that it turns up in oral tradition in all three countries. The story is set, as here, in Liverpool on English broadsides, but in Greenock and Belfast in Scottish and Irish versions. William Bartlett's version was somewhat garbled and fragmentary, so Purslow filled it out with a broadside version.

All of the English broadsides are without imprint, but one in the Crampton Collection (British Library, 11621.h.11, vol. 8, no. 482) is probably by Disley of London. We have seen no versions earlier than c.1840, but there is in *Songs from the Manuscript Collection of John Bell*, ed. by D. I. Harker (Durham: Surtees Society, 1985), p. 338, a corrupted Scottish border version, 'The Bunch of Nuts', dating from about that period, which would indicate that the song is somewhat older than that date. The plot and style are typical of pieces from the middle of the eighteenth century.

Modern versions: FTRAX219 *Bottoms Up: Songs Miss Pringle Never Taught Us* (Frank Purslow and John Pearse, 'Bunch of Nuts'); Wild Goose WGS332 *Tide of Change* (Tom Brown).

The Country Carrier
Roud 1400

As 'My Rattling Mare and I', this song was written and sung by the ubiquitous Harry Clifton (1832–72), one of the greatest entertainers of the 1860s, many of whose songs still linger in the folk repertoire. It was written c.1867 as a follow-up to his popular song 'My Old Wife' (c.1866), which has a similar chorus and the same tune. Judging by the last two lines of the chorus, we can conjecture that by 1867 Clifton's marital relations had taken a turn for the worse. A possible cause of this is also hinted at in a slightly later piece, 'My Mother-in-Law'. The cover of the sheet music for 'My Old Wife' has the 35-year-old Clifton in character as an old man, complete with walking stick; while on the cover of 'My Rattling Mare and I', he is the jaunty young driver of a carrier's cart.

Not only is Henry Norris's tune almost note for note Clifton's original, it is even in the same key. Oral versions are also found in Scottish and Irish collections of the early twentieth century. Clifton constantly toured Britain, popularizing his songs – no wonder he only lived to the age of forty. He was reputed to have written more than five hundred songs, and even if this is an exaggeration, he certainly packed a lot into his short life.

Versions from tradition: British Library, Archival Sound Recordings, Traditional Music in England, 1CDR0009333 C1009/8 (John Hodson, Yorkshire, 'The Rattling Old Black Mare').

Modern recording of the *Wanton Seed* version: Forest Tracks FTCD205 *There's a Clear Crystal Fountain* (Gwilym Davies).

The Crafty Maid's Policy
Roud 1624

Scarce in oral tradition, Mrs Russell could only recall parts of three stanzas of this song, although Sharp had a Somerset version that conveys more than enough of the joke in its six stanzas (see Cecil Sharp's *Collection of English Folk Songs*, ed. by Maud Karpeles, 2 vols (London: Oxford University Press, 1974), II, 55). Purslow completed his text from a Disley broadside, Mrs Russell's text comprising parts of stanzas 1 and 4, and the whole of stanza 5.

The same eight stanzas were printed by Pitts of London and others early in the nineteenth century, but there is a much longer version from the late eighteenth century, titled *The Frolicsome Maiden; or, The Gentleman Outwitted* (Bodleian Library, Firth c.18(52)), in which the girl agrees to take the matter to a Justice of the Peace, who rules that the girl should keep the horse. The ballad has been much improved by both shortenings. The tricking of a gentleman by a young girl was a popular subject in the eighteenth century and beyond.

Modern versions: Topic TSDL216 (reissued as Fellside FECD151) *Lovely on the Water* (Frankie Armstrong) and Topic 70-2 *Three Score and Ten* (Frankie Armstrong).

Creeping Jane

Roud 1012 (Laws Q 23)

This song has all the hallmarks of fiction about it. Firstly, the name of the racehorse is one of the most common from the eighteenth century to the nineteenth; secondly, horse-racing songs based on fact usually mention the places and people involved, which this one does not; and, thirdly, the events described set up a scenario more at home in a novel or film. The standard broadside text was first printed in northern England and picked up by the London printers c.1850. The earliest copy I have seen was printed by Swindells of Manchester, who was printing c.1810–50, and George Walker of Durham had it in his 1839 catalogue. It is not surprising to find such a stirring song adapted to fit the prowess of other racehorses. There is, however, some suggestion that Creeping Jane was actually the famous mare Yorkshire Jenny, which won the King's Plate at Newmarket in April 1764.

Since the first edition of *The Wanton Seed* was printed, the folk world has had access to the inspirational rendition by Joseph Taylor of Saxby-All-Saints, Lincolnshire, recorded by Percy Grainger in 1906, a month after Hammond noted down Sam Dawe's version.

Versions from tradition: Topic TSCD 658 *A story I'm just about to tell* (Joseph Taylor, Lincolnshire) and Topic 70-1 *Three Score and Ten* (Joseph Taylor); Musical Traditions MTCD351 *A Country Life* (Bill Smith, Shropshire, 'Creeping Jane').

The Cruel Ship's Carpenter

Roud 15 (Laws P36)

'Jonah ballads' like this one appear to have been widespread across northern Europe. They can be traced back in Britain at least to the seventeenth century and were probably originally based upon their continental equivalents. The motif of a dead lover's ghost approaching the ship in which the offending lover is sailing and wreaking vengeance upon him can be found in a number of British ballads, such as 'Captain Glen' (*Roud 478, Laws K22*), and 'The Sailor's Tragedy' (Roud 568, Laws P34) in this volume. Useful notes on the continental relatives can be found in the notes to 'Brown Robyn's Confession' (*Child 57*) *in The English and Scottish Popular Ballads*, but the Child ballad is quite possibly a Peter Buchan composition based on Danish versions.

The ballad given here first appeared on broadsides in the middle of the eighteenth century as *The Gosport Tragedy*, with up to thirty-five stanzas. Even in this lengthy form, it entered oral tradition in both Britain and America, but it is the widely printed version given here, prudently trimmed down to eleven stanzas by a broadside writer c.1790, that became immensely popular on both sides of the Atlantic. Like other broadside ballads (such as 'Lord Lovel' and 'William and Dinah'), it was burlesqued and sung in the early nineteenth-century supper rooms, as 'Molly the Betrayed'. Alfred Stride's title 'Pretty Polly' is sometimes used for American versions.

Versions from tradition: Topic TSCD667 *It fell on a day, a bonny summer's day* (Harry Cox, Norfolk, 'In Worcester City'); Topic TSCD511 *Now Is the Time for Fishing* (Sam Larner, Norfolk, 'The Ghost Ship'); Musical Traditions MTCD346 *The Brazil Family: Down by the Old Riverside* (Weenie Brazil and Danny Brazil, Gloucester); Musical Traditions MTCD307 *Band of Gold* (Denny Smith and Wiggy Smith, Gloucestershire, 'The Ship Carpenter's Mate'); Musical Traditions MTCD317 *Chainmaker* (George Dunn,

Warwickshire); Topic TSCD673T *Good People, Take Warning* (Sam Larner, Norfolk, 'Pretty Polly').

The Cuckoo
Roud 413

This is a very old and widespread female lament, regretting unfaithful love. Like many similar items, it has undergone much alteration in oral tradition over the centuries. Even broadside versions from c.1800 suggest the influence of oral tradition. Strangely, almost all of the oral versions seem to relate to the 1802 garland version *The Forsaken Nymph* printed by Robertson of Glasgow (British Library, 11606.aa.23.78.(4.)), ignoring the broadside version printed by Evans, Pitts, and Catnach in London. The song has become well established in North America, where it has hybridized with a number of other songs.

Stanza 4 here is a commonplace not found in any other version (see 'Flash Company' in this book). The second half of stanza 5 and the first half of stanza 6 have been added from a version collected by Alfred Williams from Mrs Alice Barnett of Quenington, Gloucestershire, and the first half of stanza 6 again occurs in no other version. By this collation, Purslow has made what was already an unusual version even more unusual.

Versions from tradition: Topic TSCD666 *You lazy lot of boneshakers* (Turp Brown, Hampshire, two stanzas in 'Abroad as I Was Walking'); Musical Traditions MTCD320 *Here's Luck to a Man* (Minty Smith, Surrey, 'The Cuckoo Is a Merry Bird'); Musical Traditions MTCD306 *Put a Bit of Powder on it, Father* (Walter Pardon, Norfolk); Veteran VT120 *A Sweet Country Life* (Bob Lewis, Sussex); FTRAX015 *A Blacksmith Courted Me* (Charlie Phillips); Topic TSCD672D *I'm a Romany Rai* (Carolyne Hughes, Dorset).

The Dandy Husband
Roud 15129

Here is a good example of someone remembering a fragment of a popular song from his youth. This song and its companion piece, 'The Dandy Wife', were both common on broadsides in the early nineteenth century. In fact, I have counted twenty-five different songs of this period in my broadside index that start with the word 'dandy'. In the eighteenth century, 'dandy' was used as a noun, meaning a well-heeled man who dressed extravagantly or in an effeminate way. It then evolved as an adjective meaning eccentric, and in America it took on an even wider sense as a synonym for 'good', as in the expression 'fine and dandy'.

Versions from tradition: Musical Traditions MTCD306 *Put a Bit of Powder on it, Father* (Walter Pardon, Norfolk, 'The Dandy Man').

The Darling Boy
Roud 1452

Looking at longer oral versions it is clear that this song is closely related to 'If I Was a Blackbird' in this volume. One possibility is that they both evolved from a single earlier broadside ballad. The only oral versions of 'The Darling Boy' come from Somerset and these very likely derive from broadsides printed in Bristol by Collard or Clouter in the early nineteenth century. The sixth stanza in this and Mrs Overd's version (*Still Growing*, p. 69) occurs in none of the broadsides and is one of those ancient commonplaces found in such songs. Purslow added stanza 5 from a broadside and, perhaps not surprisingly, chose to place it in the same position it occupies in Mrs Overd's version – as opposed to in the broadsides where it comprises the third stanza.

Modern recording of a version close to Mrs Gulliver's: Wild Goose WGS322CD *Floating Verses* (Mary Humphreys, based on the version of Mrs Overd of Langport, Somerset).

The Death of Parker
Roud 1032
Purslow's note gives the salient facts: 'In April 1797 the Channel fleet mutinied at Spithead due to grievances over pay, prize money, and shipboard conditions generally. Their demands were met by the government. Shortly afterwards the North Sea fleet mutinied at the Nore, making bigger demands still. Richard Parker was the leader of this mutiny and proclaimed himself "President of the Floating Republic". The fleet blockaded the Thames and fired on ships. About fifteen thousand troops were sent against the mutineers, and the ships were bombarded by Tilbury Fort. The mutiny collapsed and Parker was hanged at the yardarm on 30 June 1797. The song presumably appeared shortly afterwards. It exists in two versions, one obviously deriving from the other. The story of the exhumation of Parker's body by his widow only appears in one of them, and this is most probably the original song. The other one substitut[es] verses describing the widow's distress and hoping that Parker's soul may be shining in Heaven, etc., verses, to judge from the attempts at rhyming, which are the work of a second-rate hack.'

Both versions were printed within ten years of the event, but the tidied-up version continued to be printed throughout the nineteenth century.

Versions from tradition: Musical Traditions MTCD335 *Songs from the Golden Fleece* (Audrey Smith, track 5)

Down by the Woods and Shady Green Trees (The Shady Green Tree)
Roud 2512
Irish versions have attracted a few extra stanzas, but other than that Mrs Bowen's version, like other English versions, is almost word for word the same as the late eighteenth-century broadside *The Shady Green Tree* (e.g. Bodleian Library, Harding B 25(1754)). In the older ballads, encounters 'down by the woods and shady green trees' are inevitably of a sexual nature, and this may be an echo of those. Another four-stanza text collected by Gardiner in Hampshire is GG/1/20/1238.

The tune appears to have some affinity with that found with some versions of 'The Game of All Fours' (*Roud 232*) (*Marrow Bones*, p42).

Versions from tradition: Topic 12T359 *The Bonny Green Tree* (John Reilly, Roscommon, 'The Bonny Green Tree').

The Drowned Lover (The Lover's Lament for her Sailor)
Roud 466

Apart from this song, James Lake's repertoire consisted entirely of local church carols. During the early nineteenth century the burlesquing of street ballads in supper rooms and cellars was very popular, and this was one of those that suffered at the hands of the likes of the music hall entertainer Sam Cowell. The transformation of 'William and Dinah' into 'Villikins and his Dinah' is possibly the most famous example. Not surprisingly, many of the burlesque versions of songs such as 'Billy Taylor', 'Lord Lovel', and 'Ah, My Love's Dead' (our song here) found their way back into oral tradition and eventually became serious songs again.

The prototype for this song, *Captain Digby's Farewell*, is earlier than 1671, and *was lengthened into The Sorrowful Lady's Complaint*, c.1673. The early history of the song is documented in detail by J. Woodfall Ebsworth (Sam Cowell's brother-in-law) in the *The Roxburghe Ballads*, 9 vols (London; Hertford: Ballad Society, 1869–97), IV, 392–400. The song has continued in various forms in oral tradition to the present day, and has even become known as a pop song in America, following the Carter Family's chart success 'I Never Will Marry'.

Version from tradition: Country Branch CBCD095 *Good Tunes Enough* (Gordon Hall, Sussex, 'The Constant Lovers'). Version partly based on James Lake's: Veteran VT131CD *When the May is all in Bloom* (Ron Spicer, Kent, 'Constant Lovers').

Farewell, Dearest Nancy
Roud 527 (Laws K14)

Yet another street ballad that can be traced back at least to the seventeenth century; as *The Seaman's Doleful Farewel; or, The Greenwitch Lovers Mournful Departure* it was printed by J. Deacon in 1685 (Pepys Ballads 4.186). By the early nineteenth century it was being printed in England and Ireland under a wide range of titles, so it is not surprising that it turns up in oral tradition in many parts of the English-speaking world, in a wide variety of forms.

Mrs Russell's version has been popular with the folk revival for over forty years since it appeared in Purslow's first edition. Marina Russell's tunes are distinctive and singers like Martin Carthy have enthused over them on many occasions.

Versions from tradition: Topic TSCD662 *We've received orders to sail* (Nora Cleary, Co. Clare, 'Farewell, Lovely Mary'); Topic 12TS401 *After Dawning* (Joe Holmes and Len Graham, Antrim, 'Johnnie and Mollie').

Fathom the Bowl
Roud 880

As 'The Punch Ladle' this song was published in William Barrett's *English Folk-Songs*, 1891, p70. It was this version popularized by the Waterson family in the 1960s that took the folk scene by storm as a full-throated harmony song. Barrett stated it is 'still popular in many rural districts and dates from about the year 1770'. Under his title it appeared on broadsides printed by Pitts and Catnach of London and their successors. Lucy Broadwood published a version to a different tune in 1893 in *English County Songs*.

The tune we know so well today comes from Harry Clifton's 'Polly Perkins of Paddington Green' of 1863, or at least he claimed to have composed it. It has similarities also with some versions of 'The Bold Grenadier' (*Roud 140*).

A modern version can be heard on Topic TSCD472 *The Watersons, Early Days* (The Watersons, track 12).

The Female Drummer
Roud 226

At least two versions, this one and another popularized by the Waterson family, have been frequently sung in folk clubs since the 1960s. Harry Cox of Norfolk and Mary Ann Haynes, a Traveller from Hampshire, both sang practically the same tune as William Bone. The theme was a popular one in the late eighteenth century, when similar songs were printed, and in oral tradition, some of them full of sexual imagery. This one, in which the maiden is occasionally fifteen years old, was much printed on broadsides in England for more than a century. There are nine stanzas in the broadside version (e.g. Bodleian Library, Harding B 11(2338)).

Versions from tradition: Topic TSCD661 *My father's the king of the gypsies* (Mary Ann Haynes, Sussex); Topic TSCD512D *The Bonny Labouring Boy* (Harry Cox, Norfolk); Topic TSCD514 *A World without Horses* (Walter Pardon, Norfolk,); Topic SP104 *Why Can't It Always Be Saturday?* (Harry Upton, Sussex, track 5); Musical Traditions MTCD339 *A Story to Tell* (Bill 'Dodger' Brabbing, Suffolk); Topic TSCD673T *Good People, Take Warning* (Margaret Jeffrey, Perthshire, 'When I Was a Young Maid').

The Female Highwayman
Roud 7 (Laws N21)

From the early seventeenth century through to the late nineteenth century, the broadside presses had as one of their most popular themes songs based on the adventures of women taking on roles normally associated with men, so that female drummers, robbers, soldiers, etc. abound, the most popular by far being female sailors. While many of these are fictional, at least some of the sailor and soldier songs are based on real events. This one is surely pure entertainment, as are all of the other female robber songs I have seen (e.g. *Roud 1315*).

The name 'Shillo' is a corruption of 'Sylvia', featured in all of the extant broadsides, the earliest of which, printed by Robertson of Glasgow, is dated 1802. By the time Disley of London was printing a version in the mid-nineteenth century its seven stanzas had been expanded to ten, under the most common title of *Sylvia's Request and Young William's Denial*. Its most likely origin lies in the London pleasure gardens or theatres of the late eighteenth century.

Mrs Young's version was given a new lease of life in the 1960s by Martin Carthy and Dave Swarbrick.

Versions from tradition: Topic 12T195 *Fair Game and Foul* (Timothy Walsh, Devon, 'Sylvia'); Veteran tape VT107 *Ripest Apples* (Mabs Hall, Sussex, 'Cecilia'); Musical Traditions MTCD318 *Chainmaker* (George Dunn, Warwickshire).

Flash Company

Roud 954

Scarce on broadsides and mostly fragmentary in oral tradition this little song favoured by travellers is sometimes titled 'The Yellow Handkerchief'. The two broadside versions with imprint were printed by Jackson of Birmingham and Hodges of London, but one without imprint [See *Bodleian Broadside Ballads* website, Harding B15 (109a)] ascribes the song to Thomas Smith which accords with the Thomas mentioned in the first stanza. The fourth stanza runs:

> Here's adieu to you judges, you are too severe,
> You have banished my true love far from home,
> But the rocks shall....etc.'

The last two lines are the same as the second commonplace given by Purslow. The first commonplace (floater) given by Purslow is derived from the broadside song 'The Wandering Girl', *Roud 1691*. Purslow published a traditional version of this song in his fourth book in this series, *The Foggy Dew*, p90. Somewhat ironically the version most frequently heard in folk clubs derives from a recording of traveller Phoebe Smith, recorded by, amongst others, Frank Purslow. Traveller and Suffolk versions tend to be hybrids of 'Flash Company' and 'The Wandering Girl'. Nelson Ridley's three stanzas titled 'The Yellow Handkerchief' are a hotchpotch of five different songs. (See *Travellers' Songs of England and Scotland*, p141) Read's tune is quite different from the 'Fareweel to Tarwathie/Navvy Boots/Fair Flower of Northumberland' tune favoured by travellers.

For recordings from tradition see: Topic TSCD661 *My father's the king of the gypsies* (Phoebe Smith, Kent, track 1, 'The Yellow Handkerchief'); Topic TSCD672D *I'm A Romany Rai*, CD2 (Carolyne Hughes, Dorset, track 6, 'Once I had a colour'); Topic 12TS243 *Flash Company* (Percy Webb, Suffolk, track 8); Musical Traditions MTCD303 *Plenty of Thyme* (Cyril Poacher, Suffolk, track 25); Musical Traditions MTCD401 *Down the Cherry Tree* (Pop Maynard, Sussex, track 15, 'Once I loved a young man'); Musical Traditions MTCD364 *Old fashioned Songs* (Cecilia Costello, Birmingham, track 5, 'I once loved a young man'); EFDSS CD002 *A Century of Song* (Mary Ann Haynes, Sussex, track 14), and Veteran VTC2CD *Songs Sung in Suffolk* (Geoff Ling, Suffolk, track 14).

The Frolic (The Sailor's Frolic)

Roud 1638

Broadside titles include *The Sailor's Frolic* and *The Tar's Frolic; or, The Adventures of a British Sailor*. The few oral versions are confined to southern counties. 'Frolics', or amorous adventures, like this one, were a common ballad theme in the late eighteenth century. J. W. Ebsworth dates the Evans of London broadside to c.1779 (Roxburghe Ballads 3.435). In such fictional encounters Jack Tar usually comes off best; sailors were more inclined to spend their money on street ballads than were 'doxies'!

Versions from tradition: Topic TSCD512D *The Bonny Labouring Boy* (Harry Cox, Norfolk, 'Miss Doxy'); EFDSS CD002 *A Century of Song* (Walter Pardon, Norfolk, 'Bright Golden Store').

Modern versions: FTRAX 219 *Bottoms Up, Songs Miss Pringle Never Taught Us* (Frank Purslow and John Pearse, 'Sailor's Frolic').

The Gay Ploughboy
Roud 1639
I have seen only one copy of this song on a broadside, printed by Fortey of London under the title *Patty and her Gay Ploughboy* (Madden Ballads, vol. 11 (London Printers, vol. 5), no 800), but the title also appears in the catalogue of W. & T. Fordyce of Newcastle from the 1840s. Its scarcity on broadsides is reflected in its scarcity in oral tradition, which helps to demonstrate the enormous influence the broadside press had on oral tradition. The only other oral version I have seen was collected by Alfred Williams in Wiltshire (Alfred Williams MS Collection, Wt 443). Purslow observed: 'Like the china shepherds and shepherdesses these songs are nearly always the product of 18th century Urbania.'

George Collins
Roud 147
Apparently the only extant early printed copy of this song, *Giles Collins*, with music notation, dates from c.1780 (British Library, G.308.(28.)). The song is directed to be sung 'In a crying style, as sung by Mr. Needham'. Its seven stanzas contain only the second scene of the drama, when Collins arrives back at his own father's gate, ending with the burial and the motif of the twining branches of rose and briar, which are then cut down by the parson. The language of the early printed song is that of burlesque, which is the case with all of the English versions. Although I have seen no later broadsides, the title exists in the catalogue of Hook of Brighton, which is probably the source of the six versions collected in Hampshire.

The song's popularity in the eighteenth and early nineteenth centuries is attested by the many rewritings and parodies it inspired, such as 'Giles Collins and Lady Alis' (see *The Universal Songster; or, Museum of Mirth*, 3 vols (London: Routledge, [1825–26]), III, 16), and 'Giles Scroggins' Ghost', written by Charles Dibdin junior. The style of the Hampshire versions is reminiscent of J. W. Sharp's burlesques of broadside ballads, particularly 'Lord Lovel'. As Lucy Broadwood states in *JFSS*, 3.4 (no. 13) (1909), 302, 'George Collins' tunes from Lyndhurst are also commonly used for 'Lord Lovel', 'Lord Thomas and Fair Eleanor', and 'The Outlandish Knight' (they have similarities with the 'Green Broom' tune, too). Frank Kidson (on the same page in *JFSS*) states that George Collins is a parody of 'Lord Thomas and Fair Eleanor' – which I cannot see. The three ballads mentioned by Broadwood were all widely printed on broadsides.

Purslow's text is a complex collation; stanza 9, while quite in keeping with the rest of the ballad (and, indeed, with older ballads in general), appears in three of the five versions collated and is unique to the Lyndhurst area, from where all six versions came. For an in-depth study of this ballad and its relation to Child 42 'Clerk Colvill' and Child 85 'Lady Alice', see David Atkinson, '"George Collins" in Hampshire', *The Flowering Thorn*, ed. by Thomas A. McKean (Logan: Utah University Press, 2003), pp. 193–204. For a recording of George Blake's version, sung by Tim Radford, and an excellent study of Blake's songs and other singers in the area, along with well-researched biographies, see *George Blake's Legacy*, Forest Tracks FTCD209.

Versions from tradition: Topic TSCD653 *O'er his grave the grass grew green* (Enos White, Hampshire); Musical traditions MTCD311 *Up in the North and Down in the South* (Jacquey Gabriel, Suffolk, 'Giles Collins').

Modern versions: FTRAX 056 *The Bramble Briar* (A. L. Lloyd).

The Green Bed
Roud 276 (Laws K36)

Widely printed on broadsides from the late eighteenth century onwards, the order of stanzas remains constant but there appears to have been much rewriting and shunting of lines from one stanza to the next quite early in the song's printed life. A late eighteenth century version, 'A Comical Dialogue between an Honest Sailor and his Deluding Landlady' in *Philander's Garland* (Newcastle upon Tyne?, 1780?), has a ten-line stanza followed by two eight-line stanzas, concluding with a twelve-line stanza. Other eighteenth-century versions show marked variation from this pattern, indicating that the song had been in circulation for some time prior to this.

Benjamin Arnold's text lacked several lines, which have been filled out and repaired from a broadside. The first stanza is from James Buckland's version and the third stanza is completely from the broadside. Buckland's tune is reminiscent of that used for 'Three Maids a-Rushing' (*Roud 899*). There is a rather amusing rewrite in Baring Gould's *Songs of the West*, p186, which was eventually translated into French and published as sheet music.

Erratum: Purslow incorrectly printed 'he's lately come' (stanza 1, line 3).

Versions from tradition: Topic TSCD512D *The Bonny Labouring Boy* (Harry Cox, Norfolk)

Modern versions: Fellside FECD216 *Fair England's Shore* (Peter Bellamy, track 17).

The Green Mossy Banks of the Lee
Roud 987 (Laws O15)

Purslow suggested it is almost certain the English river Lee is intended, although he adds that it is likely an adaptation of an Irish original. The London river can be spelled Lee or Lea; whereas the Irish river Lee (*An Laoi*), in County Cork, is only spelled Lee. Most Irish broadsides set the song in Ireland, but the Cork printer Haly set one of his two versions in England and the other in Ireland. It was widely printed in the nineteenth century, but there do not appear to be any versions earlier than 1800.

Versions from tradition: Topic TSCD512D *The Bonny Labouring Boy* (Harry Cox, Norfolk, 'The Green Mossy Banks of the Lea'); Topic 12TS261 *Songs from the Eel's Foot* (Jumbo Brightwell, Sussex); Musical Traditions MTCD346 *The Brazil Family: Down by the Old Riverside* (Harry Brazil and Danny Brazil, Gloucester, 'The Mossy Green Banks of the Lea'); Musical Traditions MTCD312 *Up in the North and Down in the South* (Frank Hinchliffe, Yorkshire, 'Green Mossy Banks of the Lea').

Haymaking Courtship
Roud 855

Late eighteenth-century broadsides of this song show some possible evidence of the influence of oral tradition. At least four of them use different titles, and two of them purport to be 'A New Song'. Three of them also indicate the last line repeats, as in William Hill's version. All of this could point to an earlier (say, mid-eighteenth-century), longer ballad as a source. The language of the printed versions suggests a theatrical or pleasure garden origin.

There are several ballads of the period with haymaking as a theme, but most have a more obvious sexual content. Apart from one from Norfolk, all of the oral versions of the 'Haymaking Courtship' come from southern English counties. Stanza 4 here is not in any of the three versions cited in Purslow's collation and must have come from one of the broadsides or another oral version. In the Gardiner typescripts Purslow uses one of the broadside titles, 'Joy After Sorrow', but wisely dropped it for first edition of *The Wanton Seed* as this title was used on broadsides for several different ballads.

Versions from tradition: Veteran VT136CD *The Yellow Handkerchief* (Phoebe Smith, Kent, 'Raking the Hay'); Topic 12T244 *A Garland for Sam* (Sam Larner, Norfolk, 'Raking the Hay').

The Herring Song
Roud 128

This song was well known, as one would expect, in east and south coast fishing ports where the herring was indeed once 'king', in that it gave a livelihood to vast numbers of people as the herring migrated down the coast followed by seasonal migrant workers. The idea that the song evolved from some form of ritual is at best fanciful; it is a playful simple folk song much loved by the communities where it flourished. Indeed it has a more land-based agricultural equivalent in 'The Old Sow', which mirrors its pattern of fun rhyming in what the parts of the creature can be made into. (See www.yorkshirefolksong.net item 56) Which came first, the herring or the pig, it would now be impossible to determine. East coast variants are usually accumulative and south coast ones as given here, although I have recorded in the same east coast village two very different versions, one accumulative, the other not. Most versions, like this one, suggest a dialogue between two performers or a solo and choral response. One of the versions referred to above actually starts with a spoken dialogue between father and son. (See *An East Riding Songster*, p7, and the website already referred to, item 31). Here is a specimen of that very rare beast, a robust folk song that appears to have endured in oral tradition without the aid of print until the last century. Strangely the earliest version, which is close to south coast versions, is an 1831 text from a Worcester manuscript. (See *Songs of the Midlands* p5.) Another early version exists in the hitherto unpublished Peter Buchan Mss in the British Library (Volume 1, p117). The fact that our version here comes from Bath simply shows that the song had spread even further round the coast. Fishermen often went wherever the work was available.

For recordings from tradition see: Topic TSCD657 *First I'm going to sing you a ditty* (Johnny Doughty, Sussex, track 1, 'Herrings' Heads'); Topic TSCD664 *Troubles they are but few* (Mikeen McCarthy, Kerry, track 2, 'The Herring'); Topic 12T198 *Songs of Animals* (Composite version Richard Blackman, Sussex, and Phoebe Smith, Kent, track 15);

Veteran VTC5CD *When the Wind Blows* (Ted Chaplin, Suffolk, track 11, 'The Herring's Head'); Veteran VT136CD *The Yellow Handkerchief* (Phoebe Smith, Kent, track 4), and for a modern recording: FTRAX 219 *Bottoms Up: Songs Miss Pringle Never taught Us* (Frank Purslow and John Pearse, track 20, 'Jolly Herring').

The Hostess's Daughter
Roud 914
This ballad is quite scarce on broadsides. Under titles such as *London Town* and *The New Batchelor*, it was printed in London, Liverpool, Birmingham, and Worcester. Variants and apparent corruptions in these versions suggest the influence of oral tradition on at least some of them (e.g. Bodleian Library, Harding B 25(1323)). Correspondingly scarce in oral tradition, versions have turned up in Somerset, Devon, and Dorset. The two versions utilized here were textually quite close to each other, but Purslow rearranged the lines and altered some of the words, and in doing so made a new song – but it works well enough in its new format. Purslow states that the tune has great affinity with that of 'Bold General Wolfe' (*Marrow Bones*, p5).

Erratum: Purslow printed 'morning' for 'rising' (stanza 4, line 2), but all known oral and printed versions have 'rising'.

Modern version based on that given here: Topic TSCD426 *Out of the Cut* (Martin Carthy, 'I Sowed Some Seeds').

I Am a Brisk Young Sailor
Roud 1042
The three oral versions collated here by Purslow from the Gardiner collection are all that is known of this song. Although there are no extant broadside printings, the song is a pastiche of well-worn broadside phrases, particularly in stanzas 1, 2, and 5. While it appears to record a journey from Linstown, in Dublin, to London, it would not be a surprise to come across a local Hampshire broadside.

The first two lines here are from William Garratt. In David Marlow's version the second half of stanza 4 and the first half of stanza 5 form one stanza, and the last four lines comprise a separate stanza.

Modern version based on that given here: Forest Tracks FTBT2CD1-H *Folk Songs from Hampshire* (Steve Jordan).

I'ze Yorkshire, though in Lunnon (The Yorkshireman in London)
Roud 1640
In the late eighteenth-century theatres and pleasure gardens there was a great vogue for songs poking fun at countrymen visiting the big city and being led astray, tricked, or amazed at the sights. In some of them, written to appeal to provincials, the bumpkin comes off best, and this is one such.

The air is that set to Richard Gall's 'Dainty Davie'. This is not the well-known folk song of that title, but another song beginning 'Twas wearing gay and late at e'en', as printed in R. A. Smith, *The Scottish Minstrel*, 6 vols (1820–24), III, 64. Richard Gall died in 1801, so presumably R. A. Smith set his text to this tune. The melody is far removed from anything in oral tradition, so it is more likely that it was the text, widely printed on London and provincial broadsides, that kept the song in circulation through the nineteenth century.

Version based largely on *The Wanton Seed*: Musical Traditions MTCD305 *Put a Bit of Powder on it, Father* (Walter Pardon, Norfolk, 'I'm Yorkshire though in London').

If I Was a Blackbird
Roud 387

Love songs and laments of this sort are notorious for attracting commonplace stanzas. This one appears to be a collection of commonplaces and is undoubtedly related to 'The Darling Boy' given earlier in this book. However it originated there are plenty of oral versions mostly from the southern English counties and Ireland, but as far afield as Australia. There appear to be no extant broadside versions prior to the twentieth century.

The tune from Miss Lee is accompanied by the text as written out by her father, Henry Lee, and that given here is as grammatically corrected by Gardiner. The minor differences in text between the two generations give us a rare insight into how the oral tradition works. The tune is very close to that popularized by Irish pop star Delia Murphy and others in 1949.

For a modern recording based on the Lees' version see: Wild Goose WGS322CD *Floating Verses* (Mary Humphreys, track 15). For recordings from tradition see: Topic TSCD665 *As me and my love sat courting* (Diddy Cook, Suffolk, track 8, 'The Blackbird'); Topic TSCD672D *I'm a Romany Rai*, CD2 (Carolyne Hughes, Dorset, track 11, 'If I Were a Blackbird'); Musical Traditions MTCD305 *Put a bit of powder on it, father* (Walter Pardon, Norfolk, track 16, 'If I Were a Blackbird'); Musical Traditions MTCD345 *The Brazil Family: Down by the Old Riverside* (Harry Brazil, Gloucester, track 25, 'If I Were a Blackbird'), and MTCD320 *Here's Luck to a Man* (Mary Ann Haynes, Sussex, track 28, 'The Sailor Boy').

In a British Man-o'-War (The British Man-of-War)
Roud 372

Not common in oral tradition but pretty widespread throughout the English-speaking world, this ballad was widely printed on broadsides and indeed seems to have inspired other ballads such as 'Susan's Adventures in a Man-of-War' (*Roud* 1533), and an answer 'The Jolly Roving Tar' (*Roud* 913), found later in this book as 'My Jolly Roving Tar'. It also inspired American parodies such as 'The Yankee Man-of-War'. [See *Bodleian Broadside Ballads* website, Harding B31 (127).] As Purslow states 'the tune is a veritable patch of folk phrases' but it has been put together well and deserves a new lease of life. It is easy to imagine it being sung in one of Gay's operas. Kidson in *English Peasant Songs*, p58, set it to the tune of 'Spence Broughton'.

For a recording of Blake's version see: Forest Tracks FTCD209 *George Blake's Legacy* (Tim Radford, Hampshire, track 10), and for a recording from tradition see: Topic TSCD514 *A World Without Horses* (Walter Pardon, Norfolk, track 18, 'A British Man o' War').

John White
Roud 1641

Private Frederick John White, 7th Queen's Own Hussars, was sentenced, at the age of twenty-seven, to a hundred and fifty lashes. He died of his injuries on 11 July 1846 and was buried in the churchyard of St Leonard's Church, Heston, Middlesex. So great was the anger aroused in the barracks that the troops were close to mutiny and Colonel Whyte, who was responsible, fled. He was eventually sent to India in disgrace.

We have not traced the broadside from which this ballad was taken, but another broadside dealing with the same event, 'Copy of Verses on the Death of John White', was printed by Harkness of Preston (e.g. Madden Ballads, vol. 18 (Country Printers, vol. 3), no. 998). The last two lines run: 'Tied up hands and feet to a ladder, while the sound of the cat reached afar, / Oh, Britain, thy deeds make me shudder, remember poor White the Hussar.' A much more detailed account can be found in Roy Palmer, *The Rambling Soldier*, pp. 107–11.

Mrs Russell's ballad appears to be unique. The tune seems to be related to that usually associated with 'The Captain's Apprentice' (*Roud 835*) (*Marrow Bones*, p17).

Johnny Sands and Betsy Haigh (Johnny Sands)
Roud 184 (Laws Q 3)

Here we have the 'marrow bones' theme again, this time shortened and revamped for the early music hall by John Sinclair, c.1840. The blinding of the husband has been replaced here by the simpler expedient of tying his hands together. Various sheet music copies are in the Lester S. Levy Collection.

Sinclair was not the only artist to employ this theme. Charles Dibdin's late eighteenth-century 'Tutheree Oo, and Tan' has neither blinding nor hand-tying, but instead finishes even more simply with the husband stepping aside and his wife tumbling into the water (*The Universal Songster; or, Museum of Mirth*, 3 vols (London: Routledge, [1825–26]), I, 416). Sinclair's song, printed on broadsides, occurs in plenty of oral collections, but mostly in North America.

Versions from tradition: Veteran VT124 *In That Beautiful Dale* (Will Noble, Yorkshire, 'Johnny Sands').

Modern versions: Topic 12TS355 *Shreds and Patches* (John Kirkpatrick and Sue Harris, 'Johnny Sands').

Jolly Joe, the Collier's Son
Roud 1129

The original broadside, *Jack of Armley Mill*, sets the action of this song in Leeds, mentioning localities such as Holbeck, Marsh Lane, Beeston Hill, and Armley Mill. As the broadside was printed around the country, these names rapidly became corrupted, which could suggest later versions were being taken from oral tradition. The earliest versions are no earlier than the early nineteenth century, and by the twentieth century it was becoming quite rare in oral tradition. It appears to have disappeared completely from Leeds, since the Leeds song collector and historian Frank Kidson makes no mention of it in any of his books.

King Henry's Three Sons (In Good King Arthur's Days)
Roud 130

Probably originally a glee club song, I have heard this sung as a round. On an upmarket broadside of 1804, printed in London under the title *Miller, Weaver, & Little Taylor*, it is described as 'A much admired Song, Sung by Mr. Chas. Johnston, & proper to be Sung at all Musical Clubs' (Bodleian Library, Johnson Ballads, fol. 84).

Similar glees that tell of thieves at King Arthur's court exist from earlier centuries. 'When Arthur First in Court Began' was used by George Colman the younger in his comedy *The Battle of Hexham; or, The Days of Old*, first produced in 1789. Whatever its origins, it proved popular in oral tradition around the English-speaking world, and in the folk revival.

Versions from tradition: Topic TSCD657 *First I'm going to sing you a ditty* (Pop Maynard, Sussex, 'Three Sons of Rogues'); Veteran VT114 *One of the Best* (George Fradley, Derbyshire, 'King Arthur's Sons').

The Lady of Riches (The Press Gang I)
Roud 601

Purslow's thirteen collated stanzas of this ballad form a goodly portion of the fifteen found in the longest extant broadside version, 'The Sailor's Misfortune and Happy Marriage'. (See Ashton, *Real Sailor Songs*, p55.) Garland versions were printed in the late eighteenth century. There is enough variety of titles and stanza combinations among nineteenth century broadside versions to suggest much rewriting and an even earlier original. Broadside titles include 'The Merchant's Daughter', 'Yarmouth Lovers', 'The Lady and Weaver', 'The Constant Lovers', 'The Lady and Sailor' and 'The Farmer's Daughter'. Quite likely its origin lies in one of those lengthy ballads of the middle of the eighteenth century printed by the likes of William and Cluer Dicey. Its most common title in oral tradition is 'The Press Gang'. Mrs Tuck had stanzas 1, 3, 4 and 12 with a combined stanza of 8 and 10 here, and Mrs Russell had 8, 3 and 4. The other stanzas Purslow obtained from various broadsides.

For a recording from tradition see website: *MacEdward Leach and the Songs of Atlantic Canada* http://collections.ic.gc.ca/leach/ (Gerald Aylward, Newfoundland, 78-054 Lady and Sailor. For a modern recording see: Topic TSCD575 *Head of Steam* (Brass Monkey, track 2, 'The Press Gang').

The Lake of Colephin (The Lakes of Coolfin)
Roud 189 (Laws Q33)

This ballad appears to be based on a real event. Early broadside versions name Willie Leonard/Lennox as the drowned boy, in Lough Sheelin. Sam Henry suggested this lough, no longer in existence, was Loughinshollin on the east side of the Bann River. The lough was probably an expansion of the river not far north of Lough Beg, Co. Antrim, N Ireland. Oral variants have been found in most parts of the English-speaking world. According to Purslow this tune is related to that of 'The Bold Princess Royal' and 'The Indian Lass'.

For recordings from tradition see: Topic TSCD653 *O'er his grave the grass grew green* (Scan Tester, Sussex, track 20, 'The Lakes of Coalfin'); Topic TSCD661 *My father's the king of the gypsies* (Amy Birch, Devon, track 29, 'Royal Comrade'); Topic TSCD672D *I'm A*

Romany Rai, CD1 (Charlie Scamp, Kent, track 18, 'Young Leonard'); Topic TSCD673T *Good People, Take Warning*, CD3 (Joe Moran, Co. Antrim, track 13, 'Willie Lennix'); Musical Traditions MTCD320 *Here's Luck to a Man* (Mary Ann Haynes, Sussex, track 19, 'Poor Leonard'); Musical Traditions MTCD309 *Just Another Saturday Night,1* (Scan Tester, Sussex, track 9, 'The Lakes of Coldflynn'); Musical Traditions MTCD310 *Just Another Saturday Night, 2* (Pop Maynard, Sussex, track 24, 'William Leonard'), and Veteran VT154CD *Good Hearted Fellows* (Geoff Ling, Suffolk, track 26, 'The Lakes of Coolfin').

The Lass of London City
Roud 1554
Were it not for a fragment from Mrs Russell in the Hammond collection (HAM/5/32/26), Alfred Porter's version would be a unique survival. Stanza 5 is added from a Pitts broadside.

Broadside versions are scarce but the ballad was printed in London in the early nineteenth century by Pitts, Catnach, and Birt.

Modern version: Trailer LERCD2027 *Nic Jones* (Nic Jones).

The *London* Man-o'-War
Roud 690
Hall's seemingly ludicrous second line of stanza 1 runs 'I'll tell you of a fight, my boys, was fought in Nottingham,' which is repeated in other versions, and derided by scholars in several anthologies. However, this is not quite as silly as it looks. The original ballad concerns the Man-Of-War 'Nottingham', 60 guns, Captain Phil Saumarez, which on the 11th October 1746 captured the French 64-gun 'Mars'. Hall's 'Captain Summerswell' (Summers/Somerville in other versions) preserves well enough for oral tradition the original name. We are indebted to naval historian, John Laffin, for the above information in his fascinating book *Jack Tar*, 1969, p184. As with many genres of street ballads of the period some of the lines are commonplaces found in earlier ballads. It isn't difficult to understand the changes to the ballad over time: As earlier ships or events are forgotten the stirring lines are not wasted, and are readily applied to current ships or events. By the early nineteenth century the ship's name had been altered to 'London' and 'Wasp' on broadsides and then oral tradition gave us 'Dolphin', 'Britannia' and 'Victory'. In some versions you can actually see the transition process as they start by calling the ship 'Nottingham' and later stanzas in the same versions call her 'London' or 'Britannia'. There are almost as many different dates for when she weighed anchor as there are versions. The ship's home port is usually Liverpool, sometimes Plymouth, and where she is cruising the coast of Ireland in the original and most versions, the east coast 'Dolphin' versions (Those most often sung in folk clubs) have her cruising the coast of Africa. The Saumarez/Sausmarez family still live on Guernsey and the engagement was the subject of a famous painting by Monamy, all of which featured on an Antiques Roadshow TV episode in 2010.

For a modern recording of *The Wanton Seed* version see: Forest Tracks FTBT2CD1-H *Folk Songs from Hampshire* (Steve Jordan and Geoff Jerram, track 14). For recordings from tradition see: Topic TSCD534 *Come Write Me Down* (The Copper Family, Sussex, track 19, 'Warlike Seamen'), and Topic TSCD511 N*ow is the time for fishing* (Sam Larner,

Norfolk, track 14, 'The Dolphin'). The last is also available on MTCD369 *Cruising Round Yarmouth* (Sam Larner, Norfolk, track 25.)

Long Looked for Come at Last
Roud 991 (Laws O22)
Purslow's collated text is very close to one printed in *The Good Housewife's Garland*, c.1780, as 'A New Song' (British Library, T.C.6.a.8, vol. 2, p. 311 (no. 4)), but I agree with his theory that the ballad may be of Irish origin. I have a version, longer by two stanzas, printed in Drogheda in 1826. This is quite a scarce ballad; in fact, the two versions used to collate this version are the only British ones from oral tradition. It seems to have survived better in Canada.

As no two versions have the same title, it is quite fortuitous that Purslow chose his editorial title from the last line because it helps to identify other versions of the same ballad. Mrs Jane Wall of Driffield, Gloucestershire, contributes a half-line in stanzas 2, 3, and 5, and the whole of the first line of stanza 4, which is lacking in William Winter's version.

Modern recording of *The Wanton Seed* versions: Forest Tracks FTBT2CD1-H *Folk Songs from Hampshire* (Tim Radford).

Lord Rendal (Lord Randal)
Roud 10 (Child 12)
This is one of the more popular ballads in Professor Child's great collection *The English and Scottish Popular Ballads*. It has been current in oral tradition throughout the English-speaking world for the last two centuries, but none of these versions is older than the late eighteenth century. Closely related versions occur in oral tradition throughout a band of central Europe stretching northwards from Italy, which is where the earliest versions seem to come from. English versions possibly derive from one or more translations made in the eighteenth century. It is remarkable how quickly a truly popular ballad like this can spread in oral tradition once translated from one language to another. I have read recently of a German ballad translated into French, then from French to Portuguese, turning up less than half a century later in oral tradition in Brazil.

Miss Brown's version consists almost entirely of the legacy stanzas that conclude longer versions. In the introductory stanzas of these longer versions Lord Randal's mother asks where he has been, with whom, and what his true love has given him to eat. Usually his reply is eels or fishes, rather than a cup of poison as here, but the effect is the same. Like many of the more popular ballads, this one was burlesqued in the nineteenth century, and the burlesque survives in oral tradition as a children's song.

Versions from tradition: Topic TSCD653 *O'er his grave the green grass grew* (John MacDonald, Morayshire, 'Lord Ronald'); Topic TSCD667 *It fell on a day, a bonny summer day* (Mary Delaney, Tipperary, 'Buried in Kilkenny'); Musical Traditions MTCD312 *Up in the North and Down in the South* (George Spicer, Sussex, 'Henry My Son'); Musical Traditions MTCD318 *Chainmaker* (George Dunn, Warwickshire, 'Henry My Son'); Musical Traditions MTCD333 *The Birds upon the Tree* (Fred Jordan, Shropshire, 'Henry My Son'); Country Branch CBCD095 *Good Times Enough* (Gordon Hall, Sussex, 'Lord Randall'); Topic TSCD672D *I'm a Romany Rai* (Carrie Warren, Dorset, 'Henry My Son');

179

Musical Traditions MTCD351 *A Country Life* (Bill Smith, Shropshire, 'Henry My Son').

Low Down in the Broom
Roud 1644
Here is another of those Scottish songs from the same stable as pieces like 'The Broom of Cowdenknowes' and 'Flowers of the Forest'. Early broadside versions, the longest running to nine stanzas, are in Lowland Scots, but the fuller versions were also printed in England. By 1800, as with the two songs mentioned above, there were several quite different versions being printed, under titles such as 'The Blithe Maid', 'Whitsun Monday' and 'The Canker'd Carle'. A four-stanza Scottish version was first published in Edinburgh in 1765 in a songbook called *The Lark*, and, according to the Glasgow Poet's Box, which issued a broadside copy in 1852: 'It is generally admitted that James Carnegie Esq. of Balnamoon, near Brechin, was the author of this song.' Whether the longer versions printed in England were expansions of this, or whether Carnegie's poem was a contraction, is unclear. Interestingly, the few English oral versions do not contain these four stanzas. Stanzas 1 and 7 are from George Smith with a few words altered from James Channon's version, which provides stanzas 3 and 4. Stanzas 2, 5, and 6 Purslow added from a British Library broadside; a similar copy is found under the title *Whitsun Monday* (Bodleian Library, Harding B 22(342)). It is perhaps unfortunate that Channon's first line of stanza 2, 'I looked over my left shoulder to see what I could see', was not retained, since it comes from an earlier broadside and is a commonplace much used in Child ballads.

Modern recording based on *The Wanton Seed* version: Reiver RVRCD06 *Peppers and Tomatoes* (Sarah Morgan). Modern versions: FTRAX219 *Bottoms Up: Songs Miss Pringle Never Taught Us* (Frank Purslow and John Pearse); Mrs Casey MCRCD5992 *Shape of Scrape* (Eliza Carthy and Nancy Kerr); Fellside FECD151 *Lovely on the Water* (Frankie Armstrong).

Madam, I Will Give to Thee (The Keys of Heaven)
Roud 573
In early Scottish versions under titles such as 'A Pennyworth o' Preens' this song is a dialogue between a maid and the Devil; indeed in Chambers' *Popular Rhymes of Scotland*, p61, it has a spoken preamble that suggests the whole thing was a warning to young maids to avoid having too much pride. Purslow suggests that the English West Country version is intended for three stage performers and should include some dancing. In this form it certainly has all the ingredients of a village stage piece. It is a widespread well-known song that has been in oral tradition for at least two centuries with little help from print. It is quite possible that it descended from the wooing dialogues of the sixteenth century. (See various dialogues in Charles Read Baskervill's *The Elizabethan Jig and Related Song Drama*, pp197, 398.) The song is more commonly known as 'The Keys of Heaven' in England.

For recordings from tradition see: Topic TSCD662 *We've received orders to sail* (Johnny Doughty, Sussex, track 20, 'Will you marry me?'); Topic TSCD671 *You never heard so sweet* (Lottie Chapman, Hampshire, track 23, 'The Silver Pin'), and British Library Archival Sound Recordings: Traditional Music in England 1CDR0009335 C1009/9 (Mrs. Cograve, Yorkshire, track 19 'Oh No, John').

Madam, Madam, I'm Come a-Courting (Ripest Apples)

Roud 542

In his original note Purslow rightly points out that occasionally, because of the borrowing of the second stanza here, this song has become confused with 'No, Sir, No'. (See *Marrow Bones*, pp75 and 160.) Undoubtedly the stanza belongs here. The song is also known as 'Ripest Apples' in most English versions. Purslow has made a good job of this collation as he had access to no broadsides, only oral versions. A stall copy without imprint dated 1776 (BL 1346m 7.29c) is very close to Purslow's collation. This has two more stanzas, the third being:

> Set you down you're kindly welcome,
> If I never see you more;
> But I must and will have a handsome husband
> Whether he be rich or poor.

and the ninth:

> He that has my heart a keeping,
> O if he had my body too
> For I shall spoil my eyes with weeping
> Crying, alas! what shall I do!

Another similar copy with 7 stanzas printed at Aldermary Church Yard in the middle of the eighteenth century differs enough from the above to suggest the song was even then in oral tradition and may be even earlier. A variety of tunes and choruses have attached themselves to the text. Oral versions under a wide range of titles are widely dispersed throughout the English-speaking world.

For recordings from tradition see: Musical Traditions MTCD320 *Here's Luck to a Man* (Joe Jones, Kent, track 22, 'Ripest Apples') and MTCD304 *Come, Hand to Me the Glass* (George Townshend, Sussex, track 16, 'Twenty, Eighteen').

The Man of Dover (Birmingham Boys)

Roud 665

While there are two extant ten-stanza broadside versions of the early nineteenth century, *The Merry Jilt; or, The Birmingham Boys* and *The Bermondsey Boys*, none of the fuller oral versions can derive from these, as the oral versions all have stanzas not found on the broadsides. The strong probability, therefore, is that both broadsides and oral versions derive from a longer earlier original, probably something akin to Purslow's excellent collation (barring Marina Russell's unique final stanza).

Here, the first seven and a half stanzas are from John Pomeroy; the second part of stanza 8 and stanzas 10, 11, and 14 are from Mrs Gulliver; and the final stanza from Marina Russell. What Purslow neglected to point out is that stanzas 9, 12, and 13 are from Harry Cox's Norfolk version. There is no evidence that either of the Dorset versions had the repeats, but most versions do and Purslow sensibly adapted the tune accordingly.

Version from tradition: FTRAX 019 *The Bald-Headed End of the Broom* (Harry Cox, Norfolk, 'Birmingham Boys').

Modern version: Wild Goose WGS306 *Prevailing Winds* (Barbara Brown, track 12).

Mathew the Miller

Roud 1050

The seduction of a maid by progressively touching various parts of her body, usually starting with her toe, in a catalogue of stanzas is an ancient theme in traditional song (see <http://www.mustrad.org.uk/articles/dungheap.htm> article 14 for a history of the theme). All of the songs that use this theme are of a bawdy nature (unless bowdlerized). Ed Cray in *The Erotic Muse*, p. 320 ff., gives detail of variants of our song, including 'Billy Go Leary; or, I Clapped My Hand on Her Thigh, A Very Celebrated Flash Song', from an 1838 London chapbook. Even earlier than this is an 1819 version, 'Billy Gillery', in *Songs from the Manuscript Collection of John Bell*, ed. D. I. Harker (Durham: Surtees Society, 1985), p. 204. We need therefore look no further for the origin of 'I go leer' in John Hallett's version.

Purslow was of the opinion that the song, not just the theme, was at least of the seventeenth century and I see no reason to dispute this. William Chappell, in *Popular Music of the Olden Time*, 2 vols (London: Cramer, Beale, & Chappell, [1855–59]), II, 750, calls it 'The Derbyshire Miller' and gives a fragment with a tune called 'The Corn Grinds Well'. It has also survived to more recent times in oral tradition in Dorset, Somerset, and Gloucestershire and The Yetties of Dorset gave it a new lease of life on the folk scene of the 1960s.

Versions from tradition: Helion Bumpstead NLCD5 *Lavenham* (Sid Hollicks, Suffolk, 'Tippertoe-Billygo-Lairyo').

The Merry Cuckold (Our Goodman)

Roud 114 (Child 274)

This is an ancient song with almost worldwide analogues. For analogues and history, see *The English and Scottish Popular Ballads* and Bronson's *Traditional Tunes of the Child Ballads*. Enough eighteenth-century English broadsides exist to suggest the song was popular at that period, and versions were also published in Scotland about the same time.

Purslow in his original notes referred to versions in which the wife is punished and also some that have a bawdy ending. Cuckoldry has long been a popular theme in balladry, invariably treated in a humorous way, as here. The Dubliners took a version, 'Seven Nights Drunk', into the British pop charts in 1967.

Versions from tradition: Topic TSCD663 *They ordered their pints of beer & bottles of sherry* (George Spicer, Sussex, 'Coming Home Late'); Topic 12T161 The Folk Songs of Britain, vol. 5: *The Child Ballads, no. 2* (collation of Harry Cox, Mary Connors, Colm Keane, 'Our Goodman'); Musical Traditions MTCD333 *The Birds upon the Tree* (Alice Francombe, Gloucestershire, 'The Old Drunken Man'); Veteran VT115CD *As I Went Down to Horsham* (Mabs Hall, Sussex, 'Coming Home Late').

Molly and William (False-hearted William)
Roud 1414

Though related to a much rewritten family of ballads generally listed as *Roud 564* and dating back at least to the eighteenth century, 'Molly and William' appears to derive more directly from a Belfast-printed broadside, *The Dublin Tragedy*. This longer ballad concludes with the lover, Jamie, finding Molly's body floating in the river and then drowning himself. Not only does it share plot and stanzas with a song usually known as 'The Lily-White Hand' (*Roud 564*), the broadside also has stanza 5 from 'The Blue Cockade' in this volume. Although 'Molly and William' has no stanzas in common with 'Abroad as I Was Walking' in this volume, it is related in the sense that both have stanzas in common with 'The Lily-White Hand'. The broadside writers appear to have been quite adept at rewriting existing songs and mixing and matching.

Other oral versions of 'Molly and William' have been found as far afield as Somerset, Berkshire, Oxfordshire, Yorkshire, and New Brunswick, Canada. Marina Russell, who contributed the bulk of this version, had for her title 'Mary and William'.

Versions from tradition: Musical Traditions MTCD310 *Just Another Saturday Night* (Sarah Porter, Sussex, 'Down by the Deep River Side'); Musical Traditions MTCD325-6 *From Puck to Appleby* (Mary Delaney, Tipperary, 'In Charlestown there lived a Lass').

The Murdered Servant-man (Bruton Town)
Roud 18 (Laws M32)

This interesting ballad containing supernatural elements has often been suggested as one that might have been included in Professor Child's great canon *The English and Scottish Popular Ballads* had he been aware of it. The story certainly has very early continental versions in that it is undoubtedly based on the first part of Boccaccio's 'Isabella and the Pot of Basil'. As this was translated into English at an early stage it is not surprising that some enterprising printer's hack of the eighteenth century should turn it into a ballad, excluding the more far-fetched elements of the continental plot. Purslow noted that most English oral versions come from the south west. Some are actually in the song located in Bruton, Somerset, only twenty miles away from Bridgwater, the likely setting for the original ballad. American versions, mostly longer and earlier than English versions, set it in Bridgewater. From these very full American versions I have attempted a reconstruction of what the original ballad might have looked like. (See *Musical Traditions* website, Dungheap Articles, 21.) In the same article I present evidence that the original ballad may have been printed in Bristol as it has text in common with a similar Bristol ballad. It is perhaps worth noting that the average length of the eleven English versions (excluding collations) is about seven stanzas, whereas the average length of twenty-one sample American versions is twelve stanzas. The fullest version of twenty-two stanzas comes from western New York State in the *Stevens-Douglass Manuscript*. It dates from the early years of the nineteenth century. (See *A Pioneer Songster*, p63).

For a modern recording see: FTRAX 056 *The Bramble Briar* (A. L. Lloyd, track 1 'The Bramble Briar'). For a recording from tradition see: Topic TSCD672D *I'm a Romany Rai*, CD2 (Carolyne Hughes, Dorset, track 14, 'The Brake of Briars').

My Good Old Man (Good Old Man)
Roud 240

This song and similar comic husband and wife dialogues seem to have been popular in earlier centuries and were probably a staple attraction at rural entertainments. This particular dialogue has an ancient pedigree reaching back at least to the seventeenth century. P Brooksby printed a version c1674 'The Jealous Old Dotard; or, The Discovery of Cuckoldry' (Roxburghe Ballads, Volume 8, p198). The theme of cuckoldry has long been popular in broadside ballads as has the related theme of laments of young wives married to old men in our next song which has a similar pedigree. Though not common in oral tradition 'My Good Old Man' has been found just as often in North America as in England.

For recordings from tradition see: Musical Traditions MTCD306 *Put a bit of powder on it, father* (Walter Pardon, Norfolk, track 20, 'Up the Chimney Pot'), and Rounder CD1800 *Ballad Legacy* (Texas Gladden, Virginia, track 20, 'My Loving Old Husband).

My Husband's Got No Courage in Him (O Dear O)
Roud 870

Understandably, this song does not appear in many published collections, but it has been found in oral tradition in England and Scotland. In the more liberal-minded mid-twentieth century it was pounced upon by singers of the folk revival and popularized by the likes of A. L. Lloyd and Frankie Armstrong. Like the preceding song, it goes back to at least the seventeenth century, when it was printed in different versions. As *The Scolding Wife's Vindication* of c.1689 (Roxburghe Ballads 2.410–411), it was printed by P. Brooksby and partners; but even that version was based upon an earlier ballad, Martin Parker's *A Pennyworth of Good Counsell*, perhaps of c.1620 (Roxburghe Ballads 1.312–313). Unlike the previous song, which seems to owe its longevity more to oral tradition, this one continued to be revised by broadside writers and reprinted right into the nineteenth century (e.g., Bodleian Library, Johnson Ballads, 1474).

Mrs Steer's first stanza lacked the second line but had an extra line at the end: 'And all her conversation was, / My husband's got no courage in him'.

Modern versions: Topic TSCD491 *Life and Limb* (Martin Carthy, 'O Dear O').

My Jolly Roving Tar (The Jolly Roving Tar)
Roud 913 (Laws O 27)

A happy coincidence no doubt, this broadside ballad was actually printed as an 'Answer' to 'In A British Man O' War' given earlier in this book. Versions were printed all over the British Isles from the early nineteenth century onwards, but oral versions are pretty scarce. It turned up in England, Northern Ireland and even reached as far as Nova Scotia. Most broadsides set it in London as here but a Newcastle printing set it in Liverpool. Rather oddly Mrs Seale's version starts off in London but Susan in the final stanza waves goodbye to the maids of Liverpool.

For a modern recording see: Fellside FECD216 *Fair England's Shore* (Peter Bellamy, track 24, 'Jolly Roving Tar').

Nancy (Beautiful Nancy II)
Roud 1646

What an interesting study this scarce late eighteenth century ballad makes! Purslow has collated the two versions. The first stanza is Garrett's, 4 and 5 are Blake's and the rest are mixtures of the two versions. What is interesting is Garrett's four-stanza version is almost verbatim the Pitts broadside 'Down in Yonder Valley', and Blake's six-stanza version is equally close to the Evans broadside 'Beautiful Nancy' both printed in London c1810. Another printing is by Robertson of Glasgow in 1802. Like many of the other 'Beautiful Nancy' ballads it is a product of the late eighteenth century pleasure gardens. It was print-ed at that time in a songster called 'Cupid's Magazine'. Other fragments turned up in Hampshire and Bob Copper recorded two fragmentary versions in Sussex.

For a modern recording of *The Wanton Seed* version see: Forest Tracks FTBT2CD1-H *Folk Songs from Hampshire* (Tim Radford, track 4). For recordings from tradition see Topic TSCD651 *Come let us buy the licence* (Turp Brown, Hampshire, track 16, 'Abroad As I Was Walking'), and Topic TSCD660 *Who's that at my bed window?* (Jim Swain, Sussex, track 13, 'The Banks of Sweet Mossing').

The 'New' Deserter (The Deserter)
Roud 493

Purslow applied this editorial title because this is how it is given on most broadsides by Pitts and Catnach in London and their nineteenth-century contemporaries in other English cities. However, those versions vary sufficiently to suggest that it dates back to the eighteenth century. Earlier versions have eight stanzas, including an introductory stanza stating that the deserter is 'Johnny, a young farmer from Oxfordshire', and the sergeant recruits him at 'the Statutes'. There, 'the King's duty lies heavy on thee' and it is the Duke of York who releases him; here, it is 'the queen's duty' and Prince Albert, which is a later adaptation. I have seen no Scottish broadsides, but the song has turned up in oral tradition in north-east Scotland.

Versions from tradition: Topic TSCD514 *A World without Horses* (Walter Pardon, Norfolk, 'The Deserter'); Musical Traditions MTCD307 *Band of Gold* (Wiggy Smith, Gloucestershire, 'The Deserter'), Musical Traditions MTCD340 *A Story to Tell* (Geoff Ling, Surrey, 'The Recruiting Sergeant').

Night Visit Song (Night Visiting Song)
Roud 22568

This song has a variety of versions, made confusing by the fact that the first stanza (lacking here) can be any one of three completely different stanzas (see below). The most popular versions in the last century appear to have originated in Scotland. In the 1960s, when this version was first published, two very different Scottish versions became very popular. Harmony groups from John o'Groats to Land's End warbled away a gentle version popu-larized by Ray and Archie Fisher, and, in direct contrast but no less popular, James Grant's 'I'm a Rover' in 9/8 time was roared out in the bar rooms with great gusto. Both of these were arguably eclipsed by Cecilia Costello's hauntingly beautiful 'Grey Cock', albeit a col-lation of three different songs, 'Night Visit Song' (first five stanzas), 'The Grey Cock'

(*Roud 179*; *Child 248*), and an Irish broadside ballad 'Willy O' (*Roud 22567*).

Purslow described this version as 'too superior to be the work of a printer's hack', and I am inclined to agree. The three different opening stanzas for this song are as follows:

Here's a health to all true lovers,
And here's to mine wherever she may be;
This very night I will go and see her,
Although she is many a long mile from me. (Scotland and Ireland)

Hearken, hearken and I will tell you
Of a lad and a country lass,
Seven long years they've been a-courting,
Many a jovial hour betwixt them passed. (north-east Scotland)

I'm a rover and seldom sober,
I'm a rover o' high degree;
It's when I'm drinking I'm always thinking
How to gain my love's company' (James Grant of Aberdour)

Versions from tradition: Topic TSCD656 *Tonight I'll make you my bride* (Belle Stewart, Perthshire, 'Here's a Health to All True Lovers'); Topic TSCD660 *Who's that at my bed window?* (John Reilly, Roscommon, 'Adieu Unto All True Lovers').

The Nobleman and the Thresher (The Nobleman and the Thresherman)
Roud 19

Purslow assumed this ballad to be of the late eighteenth century but in fact it was at least a century older. The six stanzas in the Hampshire collation were part of a broadside printed once again by P. Brooksby c1685-8 as 'The Noble-Man's Generous Kindness' of seventeen stanzas. There are copies in the Roxburghe, Pepys, Euing and Douce Collections. [See *Bodleian Broadside Ballads* website, Don. B13 (70).] Through the following two centuries the ballad continued to be printed, sometimes in its fullest form, but mostly being drastically reduced in length, and it is these reduced versions of the nineteenth century that naturally became popular in oral tradition. Stratton's final stanza did not appear on any of the broadsides and is peculiar to a handful of south coast oral versions. Its popularity over the three centuries could be put down to its appeal to the richest and the poorest of society, though the scenario is somewhat idealistic.

For recordings from tradition see: Topic TSCD534 *Come Write Me Down* (Ron Copper, Sussex, track 10, 'The Honest Labourer'); Topic TSCD670 *There is a man upon the farm* (Harry Holman, Sussex, track 13, 'There was a Poor Thresherman'); Topic TSCD674 *The Heart is True* (Sarah Makem, Armagh, track 12, 'The Jolly Thresher'); Musical Traditions MTCD309 *Just Another Saturday Night* (Harry Holman, Sussex, track 15, 'The Nobleman and the Thresher'); Musical Traditions MTCD312 *Up in the North and Down in the South* (Frank Hinchliffe, Yorkshire, track 23, 'Nobleman and

Thresherman'), and Musical Traditions MTCD353 *As I Roved Out* (Sarah Makem, Armagh, track 23, 'The Jolly Thresher').

Oh Dear, How I Long to Get Married!
Roud 1647

Purslow considered this song probably had a stage origin, and we are happy to agree. Broadsides were printed by the likes of Pitts and Birt in London, with twice as many stanzas as there are here. It is scarce in collections from oral tradition, but this could well be because collectors were not interested. However, it does fit very well into the genre of 'old maid' songs – particularly stanza 3, which echoes the text of numerous other songs of the kind. Stanza 2 of the broadside refers to 'Victoria our blooming young Queen who got married one cold winter's day'; John Pitts died in 1844, so this places the ballad c.1840–44.

Old Daddy Fox (The Fox)
Roud 131 (ODNR 171)

The Oxford Dictionary of Nursery Rhymes tells us a single stanza of this widespread popular song appeared in *Gammer Gurton's Garland* of 1810. There are stall copies from the 1830s onwards. Purslow states that the song is forever embedded in our minds as a children's song in consequence of an American version popularized by Burl Ives in the 1950s. However, it was considered a children's song long before that, appearing in nursery books at least as early as 1851, and Cecil Sharp published it as a children's song in 1923. According to Baring-Gould in Songs of the West, it was sung at harvest suppers in the West Country in the early years of the nineteenth century. The song is popular on both sides of the Atlantic. A sheet music version, The Fox Ran Thro' the Town, was published in Baltimore as a comic song, c.1850 (Lester S. Levy Collection, box 047, item 029).

Versions from tradition: Topic TSCD673T *Good People, Take Warning*, CD3 (Bob and Ron Copper, Sussex, track 2, 'The Hungry Fox'); Topic TSCD668 *To catch a fine buck was my delight* (Harry Burgess, Sussex, 'The Hungry Fox'); Topic 12TS328 *Sweet Rose in June* (Bob Copper, Sussex, 'The Fox'); Musical Traditions MTCD312 *Up in the North and Down in the South* (Freda Palmer, Oxfordshire, 'The Fox and the Grey Goose').

Old Mother Crawley
Roud 1057

A unique piece, but very much in the tradition, with familiar phrases here and there; perhaps it was a Plymouth broadside piece commissioned by the very sailors it describes. Purslow omitted a final stanza which, for the sake of completeness, is included here. Also given in Reeves, *The Everlasting Circle*, p. 200, is the stanza:

> If ever we live to see Plymouth once more
> We'll make Mother Crawley's old house for to roar.
> We'll sweat her gin bottle as we oft done before,
> Maintopsail be with* Mr Fore [who?] pays the score.

1.4 *bumboat*: corruption of 'boom-boat', a floating stall of goods to sell to sailors; these boats hung about the ships' booms in an anchorage.

3.1 *soft tack*: bread, as opposed to 'hard tack' which was ship's biscuits.

6.4 *slops*: ready-made clothing.

7.3 *apeak*: in a vertical position with the cable drawn tight.

* *Maintopsail be with....*: Presumably the nautical equivalent of 'highest regards' or 'top marks to'; or perhaps wishing favourable weather, when the topsails would be set.

Old Woman's Song
Roud 1648

I find it difficult to conceive of where and when this song would have been performed – unless on a music hall stage or in a village concert, dressed in character, with appropriate actions. As it appears to be unique, we will probably never know. Purslow presented a persuasive case for it having been a family party piece. The manuscript has 'Purkiss' crossed out and replaced with 'Perkes'; both forms of the surname are found with other items in the Gardiner collection.

Poor Old Horse
Roud 515

With the horse providing the principal form of motive power until well into the Industrial Age, it would have been surprising had this song not existed. Widely printed on broadsides, even as far afield as America, the earliest known version, *The Lamentation of an Old Horse*, printed by Sheppard of London, is dated 1790 (Bodleian Library, Harding B 12(50)). In oral tradition, barring a fragment from Northern Ireland, it has been found in only England.

Purslow suggested the song may have originated as part of a mummers' play, but there is nothing in the song to suggest this; and there are similar poetic pieces, written from the horse's viewpoint, in oral tradition. Versions were used, however, as house-visiting songs at Christmas in Yorkshire, often accompanied by a disguised man wearing or carrying a horse's skull (see <www.yorkshirefolksong.net> TYG 60, for an account of the custom and a recording of a version from tradition).

The Prentice Boy (The Miller's Apprentice)
Roud 263 (Laws P35)

Here is yet another ancient and well-travelled ballad. Joseph Elliott's version can be traced back through nineteenth century broadsides 'The Cruel Miller' to a probable original 'The Berkshire Tragedy: or The Wittam Miller' printed by Sympson of Stonecutter Street, London, c1700. However, there is an even earlier ballad on the same subject in the *Pepys Collection* (Volume 2, p156) 'The Bloody Miller' c1685, which has so many points in common that it must have inspired the later printings. 'Being a true and just Account of one Francis Cooper of Horcstow near Shrewsbury, who was a Miller's Servant, and kept company with one Anne Nicols for the space of two years, who then proved to be with child by him, and being urged by her Father to marry her he most wickedly and barbarously murdered her as you shall hear by the sequel.' The bleeding nose motif is also present but, whereas in the later ballad the murderer uses this to account for the blood on his clothes, the earlier ballad places the nose bleed at the trial as confirmation of his guilt. In America it is found in two distinct types, 'The Lexington Murder' which was a broadside printed in America and descended directly from the 1700 London broadside, and 'The Wexford/Oxford Girl' which derives from the nineteenth century broadsides.

For recordings from tradition see: Topic TSCD512D *The Bonny Labouring Boy*, CD2 (Harry Cox, Norfolk, track 12, 'Ekefield Town'); Topic 12T193 *Once I had a True Love* (Phoebe Smith, Kent, track 8, 'The Wexport Girl'); Topic TSCD672D *I'm A Romany Rai*, CD2 (Carolyne Hughes, Dorset, track 4, 'The London Murder'); Topic TSCD673T *Good People, Take Warning*, CD1 (Phoebe Smith, track 18, 'The Oxford Girl'); Musical Traditions MTCD320 *Here's Luck to a Man* (Mary Ann Haynes, Sussex, track 11, 'Wexford Town'); Musical traditions MTCD338 *In Memory of Lizzie Higgins* (Lizzie Higgins, Aberdeenshire, track 12, 'Butcher Boy'), and Musical Traditions MTCD325 *From Puck to Appleby* (Mary Delaney, Tipperary, track 5, 'Town of Linsborough').

The Prickly Bush (The Maid Freed from the Gallows)
Roud 144 (Child 95)
The widespread English-language versions of this song have been pared back to the simple dialogue given here, but it is well known all over Europe in much fuller versions. In northern Europe, the story generally involves an abduction and ransom demands, which are refused by the family until the true-love comes to the rescue, as here. In Britain it also forms part of a folktale in which a girl is given custody of a golden ball, which she loses. She is sentenced to be hanged and the usual dialogues ensue, with the timely arrival of the true-love with the missing ball.

The 'prickly bush' chorus appears to have attached itself to the ballad in the early nineteenth century, as it is absent from earlier versions. There has been some conjecture about the introduction of this motif (see JFSS, 5.2 (no. 19) (1915), 228–38), the most convincing interpretation being that a 'prickly bush' occurs in other ballads as a symbol of unhappy love. It does not appear in versions from outside England, or in the golden ball tale. The ballad was dramatized as 'The Briery Bush' by R. M. Crawford in 1961.

Versions from tradition: Topic 12T160 The Folk Songs of Britain, vol. 4: *The Child Ballads, no. 1* (Julia Scaddon, Dorset, 'The Prickelly Bush'); Musical Traditions MTCD342 *Meeting's a Pleasure, vol. 2* (Asa Martin, Kentucky, 'The Highwayman'; Sarah Gunning, Massachusetts, 'Hangman'); Folktracks 60-426 *Three Maidens a-Milking* (Fred Hewett, Hampshire, 'The Prickle Holly Bush').

The Queen of the May
Roud 594
Apart from some omitted material, Sam Dawe's version is almost verbatim the slip song printed by Evans of London in the first decade of the nineteenth century. Purslow declared it an '18th century minor art-song which has kept its place in the tradition fairly well', and we see no reason to disagree. It seems to have survived mainly in southern England and the Midlands, where most of the broadside copies were printed.

Versions from tradition: Veteran VTC2CD *Songs Sung in Suffolk* (Manny Aldous, Suffolk, 'The Queen of May').

Robin Hood and the Tanner
Roud 332 (Child 126)

Most of the half dozen Robin Hood ballads found in oral tradition in the last century can be traced to relatively recent stall copies. It is doubtful whether the remainder of the forty-plus Robin Hood ballads in Child's *The English and Scottish Popular Ballads* were ever part of the oral tradition of the common people, most of them having been composed for the relatively expensive garlands of the seventeenth century. Though all of them have designated tunes it is doubtful if ordinary people ever sang them even if they had access to them. Most of these were still being printed towards the end of the eighteenth century on upmarket broadsheets with elaborate illustrations, and it is one of these 'Robin Hood and Arthur-A-Bland' printed by C. Sheppard of London in 1792 that is the likely source for the few oral versions of *Roud 332*. [See *Bodleian Broadside Ballads* website, Douce 3 (125b).] In fact apart from the two versions collected by Gardiner in Hampshire there are only two others, a seven-stanza version collected by Sharp in Somerset and a nineteen-stanza one collected in Virginia by A. K. Davies. The ballad was first registered to W. Gilbertson in 1657.

For a recording of *The Wanton Seed* version see: Forest Tracks FTBT2CD1-H *Folk Songs from Hampshire* (Steve Jordan, track 11) and for another modern recording see FTRAX056 *The Bramble Briar* (A. L. Lloyd, track 19).

Rosemary Lane
Roud 269 (Laws K43)

Broadsides of this popular ballad date from the early nineteenth century and were printed in England, Ireland and Scotland. Earlier versions, as with Bartlett's, have no indication of chorus. It would appear that the well-known 'Home, dearest, home' chorus was added to Scottish versions and then these spread into northern England and Northern Ireland. It was a Scottish version that became very popular in the twentieth century and one hears in folk clubs today. However, a version from Dorset with the chorus is given in *Marrow Bones*, p50, and further detail on its history is given at p147 of the same book. The English broadside versions are narrated throughout by the girl, but Bartlett's version changes to third person in the third stanza as do the Irish and Scottish broadside versions. The first two lines of Bartlett's stanzas 5 and 6 normally form a stanza on their own and the last two lines of these same stanzas don't occur elsewhere. Although the first four stanzas tend to be fairly stable from version to version there is a great variety of stanzas used to conclude the broadsides.

Purslow informed us Rosemary Lane, once famous as a boarding house area and street market, is now called Royal Mint Street. There is a well-known restaurant there that keeps alive the old name.

For an instrumental recording of George Blake's Hampshire tune see: Forest Tracks FTCD209 *George Blake's Legacy* (Tim Radford, track 6). For recordings from tradition see: Topic TSCD652 *My ship shall sail the ocean* (Jumbo Brightwell, Suffolk, track 21, 'The

Oak and the Ash'); Topic TSCD661 *My father's the king of the gypsies* (Chris Willett, Kent, track 24 'Once I was a Servant'); Musical Traditions MTCD309 *Just Another Saturday Night* (Jack Arnoll, Sussex, track 8, 'The Oak and the Ash'); Musical Traditions MTCD317 *Chainmaker* (George Dunn, Staffordshire, track 13, 'Young Sailor Bold'); Musical Traditions MTCD364 *Old Fashioned Songs* (Cecilia Costello, Birmingham, track 2, 'Rosemary Lane'); and Veteran VTC2CD *Songs Sung in Suffolk* (Ted Chaplin, Suffolk, track 2, 'The Oak and the Ash') and (Charlie Stringer, Suffolk, Track 26, 'The Serving Maid'). For a modern recording see: FTRAX219 *Bottoms Up: Songs Miss Pringle Never Taught Us* (Frank Purslow and John Pearse, track 21).

The Roving Bachelor
Roud 1649
This is certainly much more cheerful and closer to 'folk' than its namesake broadside ballad which is a dour warning to young men not to marry. This scarce bit of fun seems to have evaded most collectors, perhaps because of its risqué nature, so we should be thankful to Gardiner and Sam Henry for preserving two versions each, with tunes (see *Sam Henry's Songs of the People*, ed. by Gale Huntington, rev. by Lani Herrmann (Athens, GA: University of Georgia Press, 1990), pp. 263–64.) The two Northern Irish texts evidently derive from Scottish texts, providing evidence of their having long been in oral tradition. There is a text in *Andrew Crawfurd's Collection of Ballads and Songs*, ed. by E. B. Lyle, 2 vols (Edinburgh: Scottish Text Society, 1975–96), I, 175, from oral tradition c.1780, and Burns is reputed to have used the tune for his 'O Once I Lov'd'.

There are four English broadsides, of c.1800, and a chapbook version in the Library of Congress (cited in *Andrew Crawfurd's Collection*, I, lii) is likely to be older. Typical broadside endings are:

> Now the couple have got married
> As I have heard them tell,
> And the most part of her neighbours say
> She wears the breeks hersel.

or:

> So green is a pretty colour
> Before it gets a dip,
> And he who gets another man's wife
> Will surely get the nip.

Erratum: The first edition of *The Wanton Seed* erroneously states that the Somerset version was collected by Gardiner.

The Sailor's Tragedy

Roud 568 (Laws P 34A)

Here we have a typical ballad of the mid-eighteenth century which became so popular that by 1805 it was being performed on the stage as 'A Whimsical Ballad, as Sung by Mr. Moody, Mr. Suett and Mr. R. Palmer'. Probably due to its popularity, the beginning has more than once been rewritten to include the names of specific persons and places. An American broadside version, *Handsome Harry* (Laws P 34B) sets the scene in Southampton and the two women are called Kate and Ruth. A Birmingham broadside, *A New Song on the Ghost of Mary Ashfield Appearing to Abraham Thornton on his Passage to America*, is set near Castle Bromwich with the man murdering the girl himself, followed by the flight and revenge scenes.

The popularity of such pieces c.1750–1850 can be measured by the number of similar broadside ballads, such as 'The Gosport Tragedy' (*Roud 15*; *Laws P 36*), which was also mercilessly burlesqued as 'Molly the Betrayed; or, The Fog-Bound Vessel'. These ballads, in which a guilty lover is haunted aboard a ship, are collectively referred to as 'Jonah ballads'.

The collated text here comes largely from George Blake's version, with three stanzas each from Sam Gregory and an unnamed old man in Marlborough Workhouse, the remaining stanzas being a mixture of all three versions.

Modern recording of George Blake's version: Forest Tracks FTCD209 *George Blake's Legacy* (Tim Radford, 'I am a Sailor').

Seven Months I've Been Married

Roud 1650

A young girl's complaint on being married to an old man is a common theme on broadsides (see also 'My Husband's Got No Courage in Him' in this book). An early eighteenth-century broadside version of Frank Phillips's song, titled *The Complaining Maid* (Roxburghe Ballads 3.560), sets it out as a dialogue, with the wife having the first stanza, the old husband the next two, and the 'married maid' the final three. Frank Phillips's version gives the whole song to the girl, as do later broadsides titled *The Unhappy Bride* (e.g. Bodleian Library, Harding B 25(1971)). The only other recorded oral version was sung by LaRena Clark of Ontario, Canada (see Edith Fowke and Jay Rahn, *A Family Heritage: The Story and Songs of LaRena Clark* (Calgary: University of Calgary Press, 1994), p. 106.)

Seventeen Come Sunday

Roud 277 (Laws O 17)

Here is another of those popular ballads widespread in the English-speaking world. The earlier broadside versions, *The Maid and the Soldier*, printed by Pitts, Catnach, and their contemporaries, have ten stanzas. Later printings, of nine stanzas, have the 'Seventeen Come Sunday' title, sometimes commencing 'I'm...'.

The earlier versions have a different ending. In answer to the girl's request that they should be married, the soldier replies:

I have a wife she is my own,
And how can I disdain her,
And every town that I go through
A girl if I can find her.

I'll go to bed quite late at night,
Rise early in the morning,
The bugle horn is my delight,
And the hautboy is my darling.

Of sketches I have got enough
And money in my pocket,
And what care I for any one,
It's of the girls I got it.

hautboy: an earlier form of oboe. sketches: probably an old slang term for (some form of) money.

It would appear that happy endings were more saleable towards the middle of the century (see Bodleian Library, Harding B 25(1185), Harding B 11(1732), for an earlier and a later version, respectively). The original must date to at least the late eighteenth century because Burns used it as a model for his 'A Waukrife Minnie'.

Several other songs, such as 'The Brewer Laddie' (*Roud 867*; *Marrow Bones*, p. 13), appear to be related. One could almost say the half-stanza 'Where are you going, my pretty fair maid, / Where are you going, my honey?' should be deemed a commonplace, as it occurs in so many songs.

Versions from tradition: Topic TSCD660 *Who's that at my bed window?* (Bob Hart, Suffolk); Topic 12T157 Folk Songs of Britain, vol. 1: *Songs of Courtship* (Seamus Ennis, Dublin, 'As I Roved Out'); Musical Traditions MTCD305 *Put a Bit of Powder on it, Father* (Walter Pardon, Norfolk); Musical Traditions MTCD326 *From Puck to Appleby* (Mary Delaney, Tipperary, 'New Ross Town'); Veteran VTD148CD *A Shropshire Lad* (Fred Jordan, Shropshire, 'The Field of Barley'); Veteran VT154CD *Good Hearted Fellows* (Jumbo Brightwell, Suffolk); Musical Traditions MTCD353 *As I Roved Out* (Sarah Makem, Co. Armagh, 'As I Roved Out'); Topic TSCD672D *I'm a Romany Rai* (Charlie Scamp, Kent, 'How old are you, my pretty fair maid?'; Carolyne Hughes, Dorset, 'Flash Girls and Airy').

Sheffield Park
Roud 18833
The earliest extant version 'The Unfortunate Maid' was printed in a garland 'The Choice Spirit's Delight' in the middle of the eighteenth century (BL 11621 e 2.3.1). However some of the more flowery stanzas (our final two here) can be found in 'The Deceased Maiden Lover' printed by various printers c1670 (See, e.g., *Pepys*, Volume 3, p124.) and in 'The Constant Lady and false-hearted Squire, being a Relation of a Knight's Daughter near Woodstock Town in Oxfordshire' c1686 (See *Pepys*, Volume 5, p285.) Eighteenth century

versions, however, do not contain these stanzas, and therefore were likely added onto 'Sheffield Park' sometime later. It continued to be printed in London, Birmingham, Hull and Newcastle during the nineteenth century. [See *Bodleian Broadside Ballads* website, Harding, B15 (281b).] Most oral versions come from southern England but as one would expect it has some currency in and around Sheffield.

For recordings from tradition see: Topic TSCD673T *Good People, Take Warning* CD1 (Ben Butcher, Hampshire, track 6, 'In Sheffield Park'), and Musical Traditions MTCD312 *Up in the North and Down in the South* (Frank Hinchliffe, Yorkshire, track 19, 'In Sheffield Park').

The Shopkeeper
Roud 1651

This ballad is most probably an oral version of a local broadside of seven stanzas, which in turn is a drastic conflation of a much more widespread mid-eighteenth-century printed ballad, *The Two Loyal Lovers of Exeter*, of twenty-six stanzas (Bodleian Library, Harding B 2(13)). Comparing the two ballads provides an excellent demonstration of how many nineteenth-century street ballads were drastic reductions of versions printed in the eighteenth century. All of the stanzas in the later ballad are present in the earlier one – barring the last stanza here, which is unique to Mrs Knight's version and an interloper from the ubiquitous 'Died for Love' family of songs. Another version, 'Rich Gentleman's Daughter', from Gloucester (Alfred Williams MS Collection, Gl 156), has more stanzas from the earlier broadside and is therefore presumably an oral survival either directly from it or perhaps from another later broadside. The fact that stanzas 4 and 5 remain a constant in all versions demonstrates how evocative this episode of the lovers passing on the road has been.

Seven of the eight extant oral versions come from within a twenty-mile radius of Winchester, so it would not be surprising to find a broadside printed in Winchester in the early years of the nineteenth century.

Six Jolly Miners
Roud 877

This song consists of a hotchpotch of stanzas, some of which are found in other songs such as 'A Sailor for Me' (*Roud 683/1087*). Even broadside versions from the early nineteenth century vary greatly, and a wide variety of placenames from England, Scotland, and Ireland, are used, so that one cannot even guess where it might have originated. Unsurprisingly with a non-narrative text like this some versions have attracted commonplaces from the general stock of 'floating' stanzas. The song is also found in mining districts of Nova Scotia and Pennsylvania. Like 'Poor Old Horse' given earlier in this book, a version was used as a Christmas house-visiting song in the Sheffield area. (See www.yorkshirefolksong.net under the same title as here.) The last stanza in William Brown's version is adapted in other songs to suit a variety of occupations.

For other recordings from tradition: Topic 12T197 *Folk Songs of Britain, vol. 9: Songs of Ceremony* (Louis Rowe, Yorkshire, track B8), Topic TSCD671 *You Never Heard So Sweet* (Turp Brown, Hampshire, track 12, 'Six Jolly Miners').

The Spotted Cow
Roud 956

This song appeared on stall copies c1800 almost verbatim the text given here and it is undoubtedly a typical product of the pleasure gardens/theatres of that period. It continued to be widely printed in England throughout the nineteenth century. It only appears in a few oral collections possibly because collectors didn't consider it a folk song, but it was still being sung by country singers right into the 1950s.

Versions from tradition: Musical Traditions MTCD312 *Up in the North and Down in the South* (Frank Hinchliffe, Yorkshire); Veteran VT131CD *When the May Is All in Bloom* (Bob Lewis, Sussex); FTRAX013 *As I Roved Out* (Harry Cox, Norfolk); FTRAX097 *Up to the Rigs* (Charlie Wills, Dorset).

T Stands for Thomas (The False Young Man)
Roud 419

Purslow suggested this song was of Irish origin and we see no reason to disagree. The oldest English broadsides, of nine stanzas, were printed by W. Armstrong of Liverpool, c.1820–24, under the titles *Sweet John Is the Handsomest Man* and *Johnny Is a Handsome Man* (Bodleian Library, Harding B 28(27), Harding B 25(993)). Later English and Scottish broadsides have the titles *Old Oak Tree* (William Forth of Hull), The Two Lovers (Glasgow Poet's Box), and *The Inconstant Lover*. As with some other Irish ballads, such as 'The Streams of Lovely Nancy' (*Roud 688*), Liverpool has, unsurprisingly, been the likely port of entry.

The version of the text given here should be considered that of Robert King of Castle Eaton, Wiltshire (Alfred Williams MS Collection, Wt 342), as it follows his six-stanza form, with amendments from Alfred Porter's four-stanza text. The reference to 'the cuckoo's nest' in the last stanza is an oral substitution for 'wild bird's nest' or 'thrush's nest' in broadsides and most other oral versions. Because of the weak narrative thread, no doubt, American versions usually commence with the first three stanzas here and then continue with a wide range of commonplaces from elsewhere.

Versions from tradition: Topic 12T157 *Folk Songs of Britain, vol. 1: Songs of Courtship* (Frank and Francis McPeake, Belfast, 'The False Young Man').

Tarry Trousers
Roud 427

Here is a simple broadside dialogue from the late eighteenth century. Almost all of its stanzas, in some form or other, can be found in similar ballads of the period. Printed and oral versions have varied very little over two centuries. In fact, the only noticeable difference between the contribution here and the late eighteenth-century broadside texts is that Purslow has inserted Benjamin Arnold's text as stanza 3 instead of as stanza 5. As Purslow pointed out, mother/daughter dialogues seem to have been very fashionable during this period.

Versions from tradition: EFDSS CD02 *A Century of Song* (Mrs Humphreys, Essex).

Three Jolly Sneaksmen
Roud 1652

Here is an apparently unique song, very much in the style of the late eighteenth century. The reference to Jack Ketch, who was public hangman from 1663 to 1686, harks back to an earlier century, but his name had lived on and had become generic for all hangmen.

Modern recording of this version: Topic TSCD418 *Sweet Wivensfield* (Martin Carthy).

Tom Barbary (Willie o' Winsbury)
Roud 64 (Child 100)

Anyone wishing to know the history of this ballad in Scotland should consult *The English and Scottish Popular Ballads*, where there is a mixture of broadsides and oral versions. Its existence in England is not quite so clear-cut. The London broadsides, while closely related to the southern English oral versions, do not appear to be the source of them. In fact, a strong case could be made for Irish versions being the source both of English versions, including the broadsides, and of American versions. There is no doubt, however, that the English, Irish, and American versions form a separate group from the Scottish versions.

The name 'Tom Barbary' has been added by Purslow, perhaps from an Irish or American version. Fred Osman's hero was named 'John Barley'; Charles Bull had just 'Thomas'. The London broadsides called him 'Tom Bright'. A version from Dorset (HAM/4/26/9) calls him 'Tom the Barber'.

Erratum: The first edition of *The Wanton Seed* printed an erroneous number for Charles Bull's version.

Versions from tradition: Topic TSCD667 *It fell on a day, a bonny summer day* (Robert Cinnamond, Belfast, 'There was a lady lived in the west').

Modern recording of *The Wanton Seed* version: Forest Tracks FTBT2CD1-H *Folk Songs from Hampshire* (Sarah Morgan).

The Unfortunate Lass (The Sailor Cut Down in his Prime)
Roud 2 (Laws Q 26)

Much has been written on the widespread family to which this song belongs and a quick online search would give one a good day's reading. One of the many male counterparts to this song is the last song in *Marrow Bones*, p118, 'The Young Sailor Cut Down in his Prime'. Another female version was published in *Classic English Folk Songs*, ed. by R. Vaughan Williams and A. L. Lloyd, rev. by Malcolm Douglas (London: EFDSS and South Riding Folk Network, 2003). p. 74, but there the girl has literally been wounded rather than, as here, dying as the consequence of a sexually transmitted disease. For the history to the song, Malcolm Douglas's extensive notes to these two versions should be consulted (pp. 184–85 and pp. 120–21, respectively).

The text given here is pretty much that sung by Henry Adams (under the title of 'The Doctor'). His first two lines run: 'As I was a-walking down by the seaside, / As I was a-walking there one day'.

Versions from tradition: Topic TSCD652 *My ship shall sail the oce*an (Harry Upton, Sussex, 'The Royal Albion'); Topic TSCD662 *We've received orders to sail* (Johnny Doughty, Sussex, 'The Streets of Port Arthur'); Musical Traditions MTCD345 *The Brazil Family:*

Down by the Old Riverside (Harry Brazil, Gloucestershire, 'Young Man Cut Down'); Veteran VTC2CD *Songs Sung in Suffolk* (Fred Whiting, Suffolk, 'The Sailor Cut Down in his Prime'); Veteran VT129CD *I've Come to Sing a Song* (Vic Legg, Cornwall, 'Young Man Cut Down'); Musical Traditions MTCD351 *A Country Life* (Bill Smith, Shropshire, 'Young Sailor Cut Down'); Musical Traditions MTCD353 *As I Roved Out* (Sarah Makem, Co. Armagh, 'The Young Sailor Cut Down').

The Wanton Seed
Roud 17230
Apparently unique in oral tradition, this song can be found on broadsides by Bloomer of Birmingham (used by Purslow to augment Pomery's version) and Evans of London [*Bodleian Broadside Ballads* website Firth b.34(307)]. Songs that utilize sexual euphemisms are very common on eighteenth- and nineteenth-century broadsides. Here the euphemism is almost cliché. Compare it with the next-but-one song, 'Young Johnny Was a Ploughboy', where the euphemism is much more heavily disguised but not as effective. Hammond's comment on the song was: 'Words rather coarse' – and in polite society they probably still are.

John Pomery sang 'Wanting Seed'. His song consisted of stanzas 1, 3, and 4 here, the rest is added from the Bloomer broadside, which has eight stanzas. Pomery had two more stanzas from elsewhere which can be viewed on the EFDSS Take 6 website under the title 'The Wanting Seed'.

Modern versions: Topic TSCD479 *The Bird in the Bush* (A. L. Lloyd, track 3); Mollie Music MMCD03 *Unearthed* (Nic Jones, track 10).

Watercresses
Roud 1653
Here we have yet another of the many songs from the entertainer Harry Clifton that found their way into oral tradition. Clifton toured the country and appears to have written at least one song set in each of the towns in which he performed. I cannot think of another writer who comes anywhere near him in terms of songs surviving in oral tradition. He wrote many 'motto songs', such as 'Paddle your Own Canoe' and 'Where There's a Will There's a Way', both of which can be found in oral collections, but his best-known song is 'Polly Perkins of Paddington Green'. He also wrote 'Send Back my Barney', the original of 'My Bonny Lies over the Ocean'.

Versions from tradition: Folkways FM4051 *Irish and British Songs from Ottawa Valley* (O. J. Abbott, Quebec, 'The Bunch of Water Cresses'); Folk Legacy CD-125 *Ballads and Songs of Tradition* (Joe Estey, New Brunswick, 'The Bunch of Watercresses').

Young Johnny Was a Ploughboy (Young Roger the Ploughboy)
Roud 17772
Common on early nineteenth-century broadsides as '(Young) Roger the Ploughboy', this song appears in very few oral collections. Three southern oral versions give the ploughboy's name as Johnny, whereas in all of the broadsides and Frank Kidson's Yorkshire version he

is Roger. A broadside printed by Such of London is at Bodleian Library, Harding B 11(2578).

The sexual metaphor seems to be stretched somewhat in Moses Blake's version, but in the broadsides it is just a single ribbon and Sue retorts: 'There are none such ribbons to buy at the show'. Despite the lack of oral versions in collections, the variations suggest a healthy period in oral tradition.

Young Johnson
Roud 12718
Unique in English oral tradition, James Rampton's version consisted of stanza 1, the first half of stanza 2, and the second half of stanza 3. The rest is added from a London broadside, with the first line of stanza 4 from a northern printing. It would appear that Rampton's version was the last surviving remnant from oral tradition, but the broadsides from the early nineteenth century show sufficient variation and geographical spread to suggest that the ballad was quite popular then.

Hurd of Shaftesbury, Dorset, printed what appears to be the earliest version with the title *Young C-----; or, a Warning to Young Men* (Madden Ballads, vol. 23 (Country Printers, vol. 8) VWML microfilm 90, no. 140). All of the other southern English versions are titled 'Young Johnson', with northern versions mostly changing the 'Johnson' to 'Johnston'. While the ballad has an air of truth about it, I have not been able to discover an actual event that accurately fits the details.

Versions from tradition: Scottish Tradition CDTRAX9005 *The Muckle Sangs* (Betsy Whyte, Angus, 'Young Johnston').

Sources

References to the first book in this series, *Marrow Bones*, are to the new edition: *Marrow Bones: English Folk Songs from the Hammond and Gardiner Manuscripts*, ed. by Frank Purslow; rev. by Malcolm Douglas and Steve Gardham (London: English Folk Dance and Song Society, 2007). References to *The Constant Lovers* and *The Foggy Dew* are to Frank Purslow's original editions (London: E.F.D.S. Publications, 1972 and 1974, respectively).

The Pepys Ballads and Roxburghe Ballads are online at:
<http://ebba.english.ucsb.edu/>
The Bodleian Library broadsides are at <http://www.bodley.ox.ac.uk/ballads/>
The Madden Ballads are at Cambridge University Library, with microfilm copies at the Vaughan Williams Memorial Library.
The Lester S. Levy Collection of Sheet Music is at:
<http://levysheetmusic.mse.jhu.edu/otcgi/llscgi60>
Songs in the Alfred Williams MS Collection are transcribed at:
<http://history.wiltshire.gov.uk/community/folkintro.php>

Other works are cited in full in the Notes, with the exception of the following standard items:

Bertrand Harris Bronson, *The Traditional Tunes of the Child Ballads*, 4 vols (Princeton: Princeton University Press, 1959–72).

Francis James Child, ed., *The English and Scottish Popular Ballads*, 5 vols (Boston: Houghton, Mifflin, 1882–98).

G. Malcolm Laws, Jr., *American Balladry from British Broadsides: A Guide for Students and Collectors of Traditional Song* (Philadelphia: American Folklore Society, 1957).

Cambridge, Archive of Clare College, ACC1987/25, Cecil J. Sharp MSS, Folk Tunes and Folk Words.

A more extensive set of Bibliographies is given in *Marrow Bones*, pp. 187–93.

Index of first lines